The Strong Woman Trap

THE STRONG WOMAN TRAP

A Feminist Guide for Getting Your Life Back

BY SASHA MOBLEY

NEW YORK

NASHVILLE • MELBOURNE • VANCOUVER

THE STRONG WOMAN TRAP

A Feminist Guide for Getting Your Life Back

Published in New York, New York, by Morgan James Publishing in partnership with Difference Press. Morgan James is a trademark of Morgan James, LLC.
www.MorganJamesPublishing.com

The Morgan James Speakers Group can bring authors to your live event. For more information or to book an event visit The Morgan James Speakers Group at www.TheMorganJamesSpeakersGroup.com.

ISBN 9781683503354 paperback
ISBN 9781683503361 eBook
Library of Congress Control Number:
2016918458

Cover Design by:
John Matthews

Interior Design by:
Chris Treccani
www.3dogdesign.net

Editing:
Kate Makled & Angela Lauria

Author Photo:
Courtesy of the author, Sasha Mobley.

In an effort to support local communities, raise awareness and funds, Morgan James Publishing donates a percentage of all book sales for the life of each book to Habitat for Humanity Peninsula and Greater Williamsburg.

Get involved today! Visit
www.MorganJamesBuilds.com

DEDICATION

For Mary Dunseath who told me that "someday"
isn't a day of the week.

TABLE OF CONTENTS

Dedication   *v*

Table of Contents   *vii*

Introduction   *xi*

Part One - Strong Woman, Trapped   xv

Chapter 1: When Everything Depends On You   1

The Birth of Wonder Woman   4

Exploding Door Mat Syndrome   6

Why Am I Surrounded by Idiots?   8

I Want to Run Away and Join the Circus   11

How Do You Get Relief When Everything
    Depends On You?   13

Chapter 2: True Responsibility   15

One Hundred Percent Responsibility Is Never Enough   25

Chapter 3: What Did Feminism Ever Do For You?   **31**

Trapped by Being "One of the Boys"   33

Trapped by "Taking Responsibility"   37

Trapped by False Meritocracy   38

Bias–You're Soaking in It   40

What Does It Take for a Woman to Win?   42

It's Kind of Cold in Here   44

Trapped in Our Stories   45

The Dirty Little Secret That Keeps Us Stuck   48

Part Two - Escaping the Trap   57

Chapter 4: No is the New Yes   **59**

Where Is Your Resentment?   63

Stage a Rebellion   65

What's the Story?   68

Screw Approval Seeking Behaviors   71

Chapter 5: Feeling Strong, Being on Purpose   **75**

What Makes You Feel Strong?   78

Taking Care of You   81

On Purpose and Impassioned–Now What?   89

Chapter 6: Fast Train Out of Idiotville   **91**

The Case of the Totally Secret Obvious Answer   92

Hey Look, Smart People!   95

Chapter 7: Who is Coming Along With You?   **103**

Your Tribe is In On the Juicy Stuff   109

Who You Gonna Call?   111

Chapter 8: Oops! I Forgot to Create My Reality!   **117**

We Liked You Better the Old Way   119

Deathbed Promises   122

Disappointment   125

Frenemies/Toxic Turd Buckets/Genuine Jerk Faces   127

Mind Your Business   129

Don't Go It Alone   130

Afterword   *131*

Acknowledgements   *135*

About the Author   *137*

Thank You   *139*

Notes   141

INTRODUCTION

Write the book you want to read, the one
you cannot find.
–Carol Shields

I wrote this book because it was the book I needed to read when I was going through one of the greatest crises of my life.

I also wrote it because I kept hearing women–*women who I find really powerful and impressive*–tell me how they feel a little frazzled, a little frayed, a little tired all the time. I also hear in their stories how alone they feel and that the most precious dreams they have always seem just out of reach. They follow this wistfulness up with a confident statement about how once they get a handle on the great burden of their responsibilities, they will finally be able to have their lives back. Over months and years, the cycle repeats with different players and duties, but their dreams keep getting deferred. Nothing changes.

A little longer and a lot longer are the same if you keep pushing your own priorities out. This is how dreams die. I want to put an end to this carnage of dreams. I'm doing this by telling my own stories and investigating in depth how strong, capable women keep getting stuck under the burden of their own beliefs. Mostly I wanted to share how to get out of the traps we willingly enter and to start living the lives we dream of.

I'm intimately familiar with these traps.

I was raised to be strong. I also was taught that to get anywhere in the world I would have to prove I was not only just as strong as but stronger and more able than those around me. I performed my feats of strength and waited for the world to notice.

When the world didn't notice, I did more.

The people who did notice filled the space separating us with their wants and needs. I added it all to the burden carried proudly on my back.

At first, I didn't notice but I was starting to bow under my burden's weight. The things I loved–writing and art–were replaced outright with a never-ending stream of responsibilities. I started to convince even myself that my life was really about "being there" for others and that my purpose was being fulfilled in this way.

But if that was the case, why did I feel so angry all the time?

When I started sharing my ideas for this book with other women, I got so many looks of recognition that I knew I was onto something. This was not just me; it was a cultural phenomenon that needed fuller exploration and then careful, compassionate expression.

For over 100 years, women have been on a path of proving our "equality" to men and demanding our rights. The power we demonstrate when we come together made our culture rush to declare our equality but not necessarily to enable it. The result is individual women trying to squeeze their way past a glass ceiling, leaving the women left behind to fight their way through.

It's stunning how individual women are still trying to prove their strength as if that was an exceptional quality. I think we are still shocked to discover how strong we are!

What if we didn't have to prove anything? Where could we go then?

Part One

STRONG WOMAN, TRAPPED

CHAPTER 1

When Everything Depends On You

I want to tell you a story of something that happened to me when I was still in my 20s. I lived in one of those apartment buildings that have all the front doors facing outside–think of a Motel 6. There was a flight of stairs to take you to each floor, a corridor out to the carport (no closed garages), and a tiny elevator you could use if you needed to carry something big and heavy.

Well, this was before cell phones, so when I did the grocery shopping I couldn't simply call upstairs to get my partner to help me with the bags. Usually, I had a moderate load of four or five bags of groceries so I would loop them over my arms and just book it up the stairs. One trip for efficiency, plus I got the tiny workout of hitting the stairs with all those bags.

I did this for years, and on good days I'd feel like I climbed Everest. On bad days–days when I was tired or had a bad day at work–I'd be all pissed off for having to do the shopping. *Plus, where was my partner to help me with all these stupid grocery bags?*

I'd come stomping into the apartment with a little anger cloud over my head. Then I'd drop the bags loudly and put the groceries away silently, –my passive aggressive protest for not getting any help with the bags.

One day I was returning from one of these trips, and it was raining pretty hard. I had my bags looped over my arms as usual, but just the trip to the stairs from the carport was enough to get me–and everything I was carrying–wet. A tiny tear started to develop in one of the bags.

I glanced at the little elevator, but for some reason I started going up the stairs anyway at a faster than normal pace. I could tell the bag with the tear was about to come apart. I put it higher on my hip and jerked my other bags closer. But just as I started to get my arms around those, the torn bag came apart entirely and a cascade of jars and cans fell the entire two stories down. I watched the jar of spaghetti sauce explode in slow motion.

Everything else scattered across the pavement, rolling into the wall and in front of the landlady's doorway.

As I cleaned up my mess, I swore under my breath and tried not to make eye contact with the people who walked by–my neighbors.

I was thinking "Idiots! Can't they see I need help? Clearly I have to do *everything* myself!"

Not my finest moment. Not a tragedy. Nothing was hurt but my pride. That said, looking back, the stewing resentment and near-blind rage of that moment really said something about how I viewed my place in the world.

I wanted to have it all wired up and "handled"–my job, my family, even the grocery bags.

I think when we know how capable, strong, and smart we are, all of life becomes some kind of performance to show the world that we are able to "handle it", little things and big things. It's a rite of passage to finally be given adult responsibilities and handle the reins of your own life. It's a potent feeling when people seek you out, knowing you have the answer or the ability to get things done. People see it, you know it, and that becomes who you want to be in the world–a kind of superhuman marvel.

The Birth of Wonder Woman

Think back to a time in your life when you felt really "grown up." Can you pinpoint it? That clear moment when you knew for certain you were a full-grown woman and not a little girl anymore?

Did you take the reins of your life, or were they handed to you?

I remember my own moment clearly. I was 17 years old. My brothers invited me to go skiing with them and one of their friends–an adult adventure with no parents overseeing things.

While I was getting used to my ski boots, I saw something that made me nervous: my brother zipped several fat reefers in the sleeve pocket of his ski jacket. I tried to not think about what I saw and just enjoy the day, but when I met them in the lodge, it was obvious how high they all were.

I slipped away to find a pay phone.

I called our parents to let them know and to see if they could help me get a bus ticket home. Then my brother, Steve, grabbed the receiver and hung up on them, saying "Everything's fine"–I had no more coins for the pay phone.

When he grabbed my arm to march me to the car, I started raising hell! After a loud argument that ended with Steve throwing the car keys into a snowbank, I found myself driving over icy mountain roads with a car full of drunk, adult males who amused themselves by hurling verbal abuse at me the entire ride home.

All this–and I only had my driver's license for a month or so!

Several hours later, when I pulled into my parents' driveway alive, I knew that I could handle anything (even things that no one should ever have to handle). I had anointed myself into the secret and very exclusive Society of Strong Women.

From that day forward, I knew that if I looked every problem in the eye with a level, unwavering gaze and rolled up my sleeves–I could handle whatever came my way BY MYSELF.

Almost every culture has certain "rites of passage" that transition a young person into adulthood. Those rites include taking on adult responsibilities, making decisions on your own, and breaking away from parental authority into self-hood.

Sometimes, those rituals take the form of things children should never have to handle–stepping in to care for siblings when parents are unwilling or unable, or assisting in work that should be the domain and responsibility of adults. These early passages are sometimes accompanied by a skewed perspective about what the boundaries of ownership and responsibility are. It gets harder to tell what reasonably belongs to us to handle and what needs a different approach.

The more we take on these Wonder Woman roles, the more ingrained that pattern becomes.

What was your personal moment–the one where your rite of passage into adulthood turned into membership in the Society of Strong Women?

Exploding Door Mat Syndrome

Imagine this:

You've just arrived home from work, when you get a phone call from your sister. She is asking you to come over and babysit, because her kid was sent home with a fever, and she is running late at work. You had scheduled time to do your own family's taxes, *but no problem*, you reflexively think. So you put all your tax paperwork into a sack and sling your laptop bag over your shoulder, grabbing the Tupperware container full of soup from your own fridge, and making a note to stop by the store for children's Tylenol and some juice on the way to your sister's place.

After you arrive, you set up shop on the kitchen table and start warming the soup on the stove. Your niece is happy to see you, but looks flushed. You tell yourself, "Once she is fed, I'll sit down and sort my paperwork." But when you take her temperature, she is *very* feverish, enough to worry. You call the advice nurse while you check the stove. In the meantime, you get a text from your sister that she is hurrying as fast as she can, but she might still be a couple of hours at work–*deadline*.

You text back that you understand and have it under control. The advice nurse tells you to give your niece the Tylenol, to keep an eye on her, and give her fluids. You congratulate yourself on your good instincts on bringing over the supplies–then you feed your niece a little soup and juice. Once the meal is over, you move your laptop into the bedroom and start cranking out your taxes.

When your sister finally arrives home, your niece is asleep, the dishes are done and you've made some progress on your taxes–not as much as you'd like, but you can finish up at home. But then your sister starts to tell you about her horrible day–her boss dumped a bunch of last minute work on her, and she really just needs to vent to someone. You are starting to get tired, but stay for a little while longer–seeing that your sister needs you. After an hour and a half, you finally go home. Your own partner is in bed already, fast asleep. The dishes are undone. You are just dead tired.

And then the long litany of questions comes from within yourself:

"I don't know why my sister doesn't have a babysitter to call when she's stuck at work. Why do I always get called?"

"I can't believe I spent my evening doing all this stuff for other people, and I come home and the dishes aren't done!"

"TO HELL WITH THESE TAX FORMS!"

But you look at the evening and can't come up with any other scenarios. The child needed care. The taxes needed to be done. Your sister just needed to talk to someone. There is just so much to do—and you seem to be the only one who can do it—or at least is willing to do it.

Question: Who is electing you to be the one to handle everything?

Why Am I Surrounded by Idiots?

While you are wondering why you are so tired and how you got elected to handle everyone else's garbage, you can ponder this as well:

Why is it that so few people seem to have any sense? It is amazing how little resourcefulness people bring to the table, isn't it? Why in the world would they make the choices they do—choices that usually end up with them needing a rescue party.

And guess who the rescue party is....

YOU!

It's a fact. Strong women spend a lot of time saving people from themselves.

Years ago, I was a new project manager at a Fortune 500 company. My whole purpose was to make sure my projects were done on time, in scope and under budget. In order to make that happen, I would leave nothing to chance. I came up with a system that ensured I knew exactly what was happening with everyone's tasks at any given time. I had a massive spreadsheet that I perpetually combed through, looking at the detail of every task I had open for my projects. It was necessary for me to have a system like this, because I had been burned by engineers before. These guys were great at telling me their tasks were "going well" when in fact they hadn't even started. By keeping tabs on minutiae, I felt I had some control–and having control felt like success.

It worked well! The engineers were happy, because I had taken responsibility for keeping them on track. I was happy, because my assigned projects were getting done. My boss was happy because when he talked to his boss he could show him a portfolio full of on time, under budget, in scope work.

It worked so well, in fact, that I brought it into my personal life! It was very exciting for everyone to have me following up on the things they were doing. And by exciting, I mean that I was frequently told to mind my own business and to stop nagging. This response confused me, because I thought I was being supremely helpful. Also, if people came complaining with their problems, I could only assume they were looking for answers (and help!).

What was most annoying were the times when these same people would show up in crisis mode, wondering how "we" were going to fix things.

Do you ever have this experience? Someone you care about is in dire straits so you rush to help them implement your brilliant solution?

Is it worse when they say "yes" to your help, or when they say "no thank you" but then continue to complain or remain helpless about their situation?

When things appear like this, I like to call it looking at the world through "idiot lenses." The world just seems to be full of people who can't handle their own garbage! The best outcome is when you swoop in to rescue them, you only want to strangle them a little for being dopes because they are so darned grateful. The worst outcome is when the willful incompetence becomes a habit and the same people come to you repeatedly, wondering how they got there.

If you didn't care, it wouldn't matter–*but you do*–so you save them, again and again.

Question: If they are such dopes, how did they get so good at training you?

I Want to Run Away and Join the Circus

Wonder Woman is getting tired, very tired. She is thinking about taking painting classes a lot these days. She is thinking about the beach. She is thinking about surfing in Costa Rica. But today, she needs to take care of business. Today, she needs to go check on her Dad who has been watching QVC at night, and now has 10 countertop rotisseries being shipped to his apartment. She needs to figure out how to not let that happen again, and how she might get those returned and his credit card refunded. She could ask her brother to handle this, but he always argues with Dad and he won't follow through.

As Wonder Woman waits in the doctor's office with her own kid to get his vaccinations done, she flips through a travel magazine to a glossy multi-page ad for a yoga retreat that includes massage and organic cuisine, all at a resort on a white sand beach. She sighs and thinks about her calendar for the next six months. Maybe they will have it again next year.

In my own life, I have "run away to join the circus" more times than I care to admit.

In just the last 20 years, I have quit my job to be a massage therapist, studied to be a pastry chef, and have even dabbled in landscape architecture. Every single time, I would say to myself, "Wouldn't it be nice to do something where I didn't have to deal with idiots on the daily?"

Isn't it strange that no matter how many times I changed course, the same problems found me?

So, here are a list of things I've tried in an effort to free myself from this syndrome of frustration, resentment and exhaustion:

Getting organized

Managing my time

Planning

More planning

Eating for more energy

Reminding myself that I am *very important* to others

Overeating

Drinking

Crying myself to sleep

Drinking *and* crying myself to sleep

Silent rage

Not silent rage

Revenge fantasies

Changing my job

Taking on whatever self help fad that promised to make me faster, more energized and more focused.

Some of these things took the edge off and some of these things made me feel much worse. None of them changed anything at all. No matter what I did, I still found myself at the center of solving everyone else's problems. I couldn't self-improve out of my problem any more than I could run away from it.

How Do You Get Relief When Everything Depends On You?

I want to be really clear. Being a strong woman is *amazing!* But if the world is starting to look like it's full of problems that *only you* can solve, I want you to know there *is* another way. You were given your strength, intelligence and talents to be far more than the glue that holds life together.

In the following chapters:

✓ You will learn how to clear space and energy in your life with one magic word–NO.

✓ You will learn how to recognize all the things that truly renew spirit and feed your soul–and how to jealously hold space for those things.

✓ You will discover how to tap secret resources that have nothing to do with you being a faster, stronger, more organized anything.

✓ You will discover the support that was there all along–how to build your tribe and select your unseen counselors, advisors, and mentors.

I have to admit, it's a little scary to *not* be the "go to girl" when your identity is built around being the answer to everyone's problem. If you are not Wonder Woman, then who *are* you?

Luckily, in the pages of this book, you'll get an opportunity to answer that, too.

It took me many years, and a personal breakdown, to learn how to get out of my own strong woman trap. I didn't do it through effort and control. I also didn't do it by being one step ahead of everyone else's thinking. Neither was it in believing, accepting, or resigning to the fact that I was surrounded by incompetence.

If you are ready to see your own life shift to one where your talents and energies are used for purposes other than holding the world aloft on your broad shoulders, then I invite you to join me on an adventure through the following pages.

Curious to see where you fall on the Strong Woman Spectrum?—take my online quiz "What's Your Strong Woman Rating?" at http://sashamobley.com/super.

Ready?

Let's go.

CHAPTER 2

True Responsibility

I have a very personal stake in this book. It goes way beyond the foibles of micromanaging others and stubbornly carrying my groceries in the rain.

The reasons for writing this book started with my heart being broken. Followed by my body being broken. Followed by the slow realization that the way I was going, my *whole life* would soon be broken.

On July 8th of 2014, my brother Steve committed suicide.

In the weeks leading up to that date, I tried everything to help him make his life work. And all the things I could have tried, but didn't do or think to do–all came up in my mind as recriminations and reasons why he went paper thin and solved all his problems with a gun.

Steve had lots of problems in his life, but he was always my much-loved and somewhat mysterious older brother. One day, at Sunday lunch at our mother's home, Steve mentioned he was very interested in the new TV series, "Breaking Bad." Had we heard of it? We were busy tucking into plates of cheese and bowls of chips and salsa, so we all kind of shrugged that we hadn't heard of it.

He spoke again. "I just quit a twenty-year meth habit."

We all stopped mid-chew and the table went silent. I looked to my mother, who seemed to grow smaller in her chair as she stared into her plate. The faces around the table were all shock and sideways glances. There was a long uncomfortable pause and then I spoke up.

"I'm so glad to hear this, Steve. We'll help you however you need."

This was not exactly a statement with a scope around it. I knew my brother had problems, but his frequent angry outbursts—and a probable hypothesis as to why he just dropped out of life at age 45—made a lot more sense. He kept his life extremely private—when he went home after family visits, we knew very little about what was going on with him. He didn't like to talk on the phone, and never invited anyone over to the apartment he shared with his longtime girlfriend.

On Mother's Day of 2014, things went sideways–starting with a phone call between my mother and Steve's girlfriend. The girlfriend started telling my mom a long story about how they were going to be kicked out of their apartment soon, and worse, my brother's chronic unemployment was making it impossible to find a new place. Long story short, she said Steve needed to come live with my mom.

My mother was 90 years old then. When I heard this story, I came unhinged. How dare this woman abandon my brother after being with him for nearly 30 years? I put my outrage on the back burner and went into damage control mode. All I knew is that I needed to do everything to ensure that Steve didn't end up living with my mother (too stressful) and didn't end up on the street.

My sister Valerie and I went into action researching social programs and housing options. I started the process of getting Steve enrolled in social services. My goal was to get him on disability or early social security–anything to get some money in his pocket so he could pay rent and buy groceries.

Steve didn't want to. He mistrusted the government. But through much gentle discussion, I was able to talk him into exploring these solutions with me.

In the meantime, I was fielding nearly daily text messages from his girlfriend. She frequently threatened to kick him out. I needed to buy time and find alternatives. We found senior housing for Steve, but he wouldn't be parted from his girlfriend. We found different senior housing that would work for both of them, but the girlfriend said she wouldn't live in "public housing." Nothing was working.

Their search for a new place continued. They found something, but they would not take his little dog. Steve wouldn't be parted from Teddy, so they lost that place too. I considered adopting Teddy so he wouldn't end up euthanized, but I feared my own dog and four cats wouldn't get along with him.

Steve said it was ok. Every time we spoke he assured me that he didn't need help, but frequently told me how hopeless things were. In an unguarded moment, he fixed his haunted eyes on me and said, "I'm scared of everything right now."

I wondered if I should take him into my own home. My wife, Keri, and I discussed how we would manage with him in the house. It was an option. A difficult one, but we put it on the table. My daily mantra was *Fix This.*

I confided in few people–everyone had an opinion. Some even shared what should happen to families that let their loved ones end up on the street or in a shelter.

When nothing seemed like it was going to work, I got a hopeful call.

It was Steve, giving me news that he and his girlfriend found a place to live–and best of all, he could keep his little dog. My family rejoiced. We wanted to know where to send the deposit (a requirement from the girlfriend to not kick Steve out) and the name of the property manager so we could get a cashier's check cut. Steve said he would call back with that information.

An hour later, I got a torrent of angry text messages from the girlfriend, saying she needed the check made out to her–and if we didn't do that, she would definitely be kicking Steve out.

That was the final straw. I told her, in no uncertain terms, she wasn't going to get a dime from any of us–and that I would be honored to pick up my brother instead, and that I would be by in the morning. I turned off my phone. I was too angry. I didn't want to hear from her again.

It looked like Steve would be coming to live with us until we could figure something out.

I went to bed in a rage, but was woken at 6:00 a.m. by a string of phone calls coming from a blocked number. I let them go to voicemail. I figured it was the girlfriend calling to harass me and I just wasn't ready to deal with her. The number kept ringing never leaving a voicemail. After several attempts, the caller from the blocked number finally left a message, which I immediately played.

It was the police.

I called back. They wanted to know if I had heard about the "incident" involving my brother from the prior evening. *Oh no, she must have dumped him at the shelter*, I thought to myself, and waited for instructions on where to go to collect him.

That was when they told me Steve had shot himself.

I felt as if I had left my body briefly, because I suddenly was observing myself holding the phone–hearing myself give each matter-of-fact response to the officer and watching myself take quick notes on what steps needed to be taken to claim his body from the coroner's office.

The moment I hung up, I fell to pieces. The days following moved with terrible slowness. To ease the agony, I gave everyone tasks to keep them occupied and fill the void–mostly, we spent our time all sitting on the couch shoulder to shoulder, holding my mother erect while watching the clock wind minutes down.

During one of those endless afternoons, I slipped away to the coroner alone to retrieve his few personal effects. I was handed the plastic envelope that contained his wallet, with the $40 in fresh bills that he never got to spend, my Father's wedding ring, and of course all the social services cards and vouchers that I helped him obtain. These are the things he had on his body when he killed himself.

The next day I drove everyone to the crematorium to see him one last time.

All through this time I wondered what I could have done differently–what if I just gave the girlfriend the money? What if I offered to adopt his little dog? And most gut wrenching, what if I had driven over immediately after hanging up, and got him away from the angry girlfriend right away? I worked the numbers over and over in my head–minutes of drive time at the speed limit from my place to his, from the call until the time he pulled the trigger.

Could I have made it? Not sure.

I examined my attitude towards Steve. How many choices I made to be opposite of him–to be responsible, employed, and to have the approval of my mother. Looking back at that ski trip we took when I was 17, how that act of self-preservation turned into a lifelong story about how I wasn't the screw-up he was. I never really forgave him for that.

Considering that bit of family history, it seems ironic that I thought I could save him, or make any perceptible change in his life that he didn't want for himself. I desperately wanted to take this grief off everyone's plate, so they wouldn't have to think about Steve's life. I especially wanted to shield my mother from her grief. I have vivid memories of the loud arguments Steve had with Mom when he was a teenager–even as a kid, I knew I didn't want that to be me.

At a young age, I got it into my head that I needed to make up for every disappointment in Mom's life. Where I started was by simply trying to be the opposite of Steve–responsible, employed, and dependent on no one but myself. I tried to counterbalance Steve's crazy, out-of-control life by being completely reliable.

A week after Steve's death, I thought I about returning to work. There was nothing to do at home that needed me there. I also wanted the normalcy of work to ground me. I didn't know it but I wasn't ready.

When I returned to work I found myself in a weird position–my boss was really kind, but others seemed to not understand that I had just been through the worst trauma of my life. I found out that during my time out of office, I was the unwitting subject of a lot of criticism. Some things hadn't gone well, and I got thrown under the bus for missed deadlines I wasn't even aware of! People were wondering why I wasn't stepping up and owning my work. I found myself apologizing a lot for not measuring up–at the same time I was angry, because *who the hell throws someone under the bus when they are out on bereavement leave?*

Apparently some people do.

Here are a couple journal entries from that time.

July 18, 2014 "*I'm tired. I 'know' all the things about 'taking my time' and 'no way of grieving being wrong' and all sorts of other comforting crap. I also know to not be hard on myself, be extra kind, take time blah blah blah blah BLAH.*

The fact is this just hurts in a visceral inescapable way. And the world doesn't stop. My instinct on Saturday was to consider going back to work. I did. I found the world didn't stop. And I saw that my work had suffered under the strain of the last month, as well as my newness to the job. And when someone pointed out the real holes (in my work), all eyes were squarely on me.

You know, you can't really wave a flag around and say 'Oh, I'm sorry, your priority suffered because of my family issue and also because I don't know what I'm doing yet.' And no one else is pointing that out on your behalf, so you soldier on. You try to fix things and fall forward.

Also being referred to as 'a rock' kind of cements that into people's expectations of being an infinite pool of strength—one you can always dip into to solve whatever, whenever. And I know I'm not, and I'm taught that I'm not. And yet here we are. Again."

July 28, 2014: "*No pretty way to say this. I've been crapping my brains out for the last 48+ hours.*

Yesterday I lay in bed the entire day, sipping drinks intended to keep me hydrated and immediately losing anything that had more substance than an ice cube. The house was hot. While we have good insulation, fans etc, heat has a way of accumulating in our little home when the temperatures are over 90. Miss Keri went out on a mission of mercy, to find a small air conditioning unit—so we could both sleep better, and also to keep me from losing even more fluids from sweating.

I felt really guilty. The afternoon was really hot, and Miss Keri is so sensitive to heat she usually ends up sick herself if she is out too much. Meanwhile, this is the first Sunday since my brother's passing that Mom has been alone. We usually all got together on Sunday to have lunch and visit. Steve called it his favorite part of the week. Mom and I planned a little drive out to the ocean to cool off, and to take a little sting out of what the day meant. Instead, I was flat on my back only stirring to dash to the bathroom and Mom stayed home. There would be no lunch and no break from her day-to-day.

I didn't have much mental or emotional bandwidth yesterday, so my guilt is here with me today: guilt that I wasn't there for my mom, and guilt that my wife was out in the sweltering heat doing work to make me comfortable."

This was the first of several breakdowns that took me completely out of the game. There was an ER trip to deal with a wrenched shoulder, an epic case of the flu, an ulcer, as well as an incident that involved being bitten by a poisonous spider. My body wanted my attention–*really bad*.

My strategy for coping with life–to be a perfect daughter, a perfect employee, and a perfect rock of strength–had stopped working. My body wasn't interested in playing those games anymore. She just wanted me to stop.

To stop borrowing against my well-being.

To stop overspending my emotional reserves.

To stop pretending that the people around me were disabled and incapable.

To stop trying to save people who never asked me to save them in the first place.

To stop pretending that I could handle everything.

One Hundred Percent Responsibility Is Never Enough

A few years ago, I held a position at a high-tech company that I was really proud of. I felt I had a future in leadership, and decided to challenge myself by applying to participate in the company-sponsored technology leadership program. I felt I was perfect for the program–I had a spotless track record for delivering my projects, as well as enthusiasm for innovation and product development. I invested myself in creating a really strong application. I interviewed other people in the program and crafted my essays, receiving feedback until I believed I had an offering that showcased my experience and leadership abilities.

I was proud of what I turned in, and was really excited to be invited to interview with the executive sponsors of the program. I didn't know what to expect, but felt very confident anyway. I looked forward to meeting the sponsors and connecting with them. I couldn't wait!

However, when it finally came time to get interviewed something was really off.

The executive sponsors seemed invested in saying *as little as humanly possible*. The questions they did ask were the same ones from the application. It really threw me–had they not reviewed my application? Between my answers, there was a lot of uncomfortable silence. I felt stupid for regurgitating answers from my essay, but I didn't know what else I was supposed to do in this situation.

One of the sponsors took pity on me then and asked: "I see you have a real strong track record for project delivery–what do you attribute that to?"

I perked up. I had the answer.

"I take 100% responsibility for all aspects of delivery, and pretend that everything depends on me. I then do whatever it takes to make it happen."

"Oh, that is very admirable," was the executive's response. More silence.

"Do you have any questions for us?"

I had nothing. I wanted to run out of the room. I didn't know what was going on, but I got the very clear sense that I wasn't going to be selected.

I tried to be philosophical. At the outset of the application process, I was promised one-on-one feedback from one of the executives. At least I would learn from the experience.

I waited a few weeks for the feedback. When after six weeks I had still heard nothing, I reached out to the program manager. She replied with the feedback in an email. It was clear that it was put together by copying and pasting from other emails. The feedback itself was 6 lines long–and two pieces of feedback even contradicted each other. They didn't even bother to edit, use the same font, or write in complete sentences! The final line was the kicker.

"Not a potential technology leader."

If my track record for success, my responsibility for results, and my effort invested wasn't enough to put me in the leadership program (never mind a respectful, thoughtful response that didn't appear to be written in crayon on the first pass) then *what would?*

On reflection, I understand that I missed an opportunity with the execs in that interview. I could have been prepared to better show off the qualities that could have set me apart from the perception of just another strong, reliable workhorse. My ability to build trust and rapport with my teams, to create strategies that garnered buy-in, as well as my knack for discovering and responding to hidden needs of the product and the people involved were all strengths that never made it into the discussion.

It stung to be passed over, but based on what I chose to highlight in the interview, and the way I handled myself that day, they made the right choice.

What I was getting praised for, up to that point, wasn't going to take me to the next level.

Confusing, right? If you are praised for being resourceful, strong, and capable–and that success is a combination of willingness to work hard, take responsibility, and do what needs to be done–then how does the conversation change to emphasize the qualities you can bring to the table that aren't primarily effort-based?

For me, at least, my life was one long string of effort-based accomplishments. It was my winning formula for everything.

I heard it was hard for a woman to get a job in the technology field. I got one, and kept getting them, by kicking ass at whatever I did.

I heard that you couldn't have a "real career" with a literature degree. I crafted one from scratch, by volunteering time testing software after work while I worked a publishing job during the day.

I heard that if you wanted anything, you had better be willing to roll up your sleeves, sacrifice, sacrifice some more, and do whatever it takes even if it means doing it all yourself. In addition to that, you'd better turn the other cheek and give the shirt off your back.

If you do all of that, well, then you are worthy. On some cosmic scale, you have balanced everything out *through effort,* and you can feel like you made it.

I thought I had everything worked out. Still, I was stewing in resentment most of the time and neglecting my well being. *But isn't that normal for successful women?*

Isn't spending Sunday nights dutifully going through emails and answering things early so you can hit the ground running in the morning a tried and true success secret? Then Monday morning you pour yourself a big coffee and get moving–you can handle it.

I absolutely thought I had things handled. I knew I was "naturally strong" and the forty extra pounds I had carried for the last 25 years was "transitional" and would just fall off when I took up long distance running and weight training, as I intended to do *real soon*. I was keeping up my end of the bargain. I was succeeding. Right?

Who wrote all those stories, do you think?

CHAPTER 3

What Did Feminism Ever Do For You?

Your silence will not protect you.
–Audre Lorde

I want to talk about Feminism. Do you ever wonder what happened to it? What image does that word conjure for you?

Is it a bunch of angry women with ERA signs, and bonfires full of bras? Do they look ridiculous and irrelevant? Do you wonder what they have to do with your life, if anything?

At the end of the day, when you are tired from work and your family needs you, do you feel that the women's movement is mostly over and that all this equality isn't worth anything? You still are stuck with a lot of work, supposedly equal opportunity, but not quite as much in the way of pay or promotions. Sure, it's not as bad as the "Leave it To Beaver" era, but are things really any different? If so, why does everything feel so hard?

Let me introduce you to a term that you might have heard before: *post-feminism.*

Post-feminism has some very specific meanings in academia, but popularly it means that feminism is no longer relevant... because we have achieved equality in the workplace, in pay, in how we are recognized for our work, and at home. According to post-feminists, women have achieved the dream!

At least that is what I'm told by men (and women) who get angry when issues around sexual harassment, reproductive rights, media representation or inclusion are brought up–issues that impact how women move around in the world, but largely don't impact men. Post-feminism fails to bring up one tiny sticking point–white male entitlement and privilege.

Trapped by Being "One of the Boys"

Early in my career, I learned how useful it was to be able to keep a poker face–especially since I was usually surrounded by men. The ruder and more sexist they acted, the less it seemed to get to me. I had a filter up that allowed every disgusting sexist joke I heard to just roll off me.

"She handles herself really well." I heard that line more than once. I started to believe that when they talked about women, they weren't talking about me, and that "handling myself well" meant I was some special breed, or that I had developed the emotional control and resistance to pressure that allowed me to work in these rough environments, and even thrive.

It wasn't personal–until it was.

On one team, there was a man who did his best to be as disgusting as possible. I could usually counter anything he had to say with something more biting, and chalk up a "win." I wasn't taking it personally–that's what I told myself. We were just just kidding around, right.

Then one day he came up with some scenario that was a mixture of sexual slavery and cannibalism. Something shifted in me and I retorted: "I sometimes wonder if you are trying to see how far you can go with jokes like that before I call HR!"

All of a sudden, the room was silent. They were expecting a response from me–just not that one.

The man came to me later, asking very earnestly if I was indeed going to HR–he was very worried. I told him I wasn't planning on it. In hindsight, I don't know how things would have gone if I did. I wanted so badly to be accepted by my workgroup that I forgot that I wasn't one of the boys at all. Or that this behavior *really wasn't okay* at work. I had willed myself into not seeing that this kind of joking *was* directed at me–that they saw me as a game to play, and possibly win. And winning meant me tipping my hand and showing I was "an over sensitive female" and definitely NOT one of the guys. And that would be reason enough to exclude me from their inner circle.

In hindsight, I see how my inexperience and denial did a disservice to every woman who would come through that group. Instead of showing those men I could "handle it," I could have spoken up. I didn't speak up because I was fighting to show I was more than "just a woman"–I was so confused about my own right to be there that I felt I needed to shut up to fit in. Unfortunately, everything was set up for that mistake to happen. In the workplace, a request to *stop* being forced to listen to sexist crap is often dismissed as a request for "special treatment," because the pervasive notion is that success means blending quietly into masculine power structures.

It's the normalizing of these demeaning, sexist scenarios that keep us confused about what a woman is expected to do, be, and accept to be successful. Under such circumstances how can any one woman alone be able to set a different tone?

Later in my career, I was a consultant with a company that had a lawsuit levied against it for gender discrimination. Here is an excerpt of one of the articles written about the lawsuit:

"The women allege that EMC's discriminatory conduct included failure to hire and promote women, failure to credit women for their experience on the same basis as male employees, systemically paying women lower wages, creating an environment hostile and offensive to women, making employment decisions based on gender stereotypes, and defaming women to their clients, co-workers and corporate partners.

The plaintiffs argue that the resulting lack of opportunity for career advancement and hostile work environment forced them to resign from EMC.

The plaintiff alleged that when a sought-after sales position opened at EMC in June 2001, she was passed over in favor of a male employee because, as she was told by managers, of an assumption that she would not "'smoke, drink, swear, hunt, fish and tolerate strip clubs.' According to the lawsuit, her complaints to EMC's human resources personnel proved fruitless."[1]

I remember talking to our sales person at the time and him saying, "She is being a big baby–I don't think there is any truth in this." He then went on to say that she didn't have to go if she didn't want to–never addressing the fact that the opportunity to do business was concealed in a place where the role of women working there is to titillate, flatter, and serve drinks to male clientele.

I would love to say I quit in indignation, but I got trapped in the idea that making clients happy is "hard" and that these boondoggles to strips clubs was just business as usual. In the moment, it didn't occur to me to question why it was "normal"– other than it felt wrong.

The clear message was that "the real world" includes business at strip clubs and other potentially uncomfortable situations, and that women in sales are screwing things up for the bottom line by complaining.

Even when we rationalize the "sex sells" mentality and tell ourselves, "it's just a game to get paid," what happens when the game crosses the line? How short is the distance between acting like "one of the guys" and finding yourself without a job because "business as usual" is starting to cross the line? And if you don't speak up, what happens to the woman who *does* speak up?

What does your silence enable?

Trapped by "Taking Responsibility"

"It is what it is."

Why does this phrase always sound exactly like "SHUT UP" to me? Especially when pointing out how some systems are broken and in need of repair. Case in point–rape apologists.

> "If I'm walking around in my underwear and I'm drunk? Who else's fault can it be?... If I'm walking around and I'm very modestly dressed and I'm keeping to myself and someone attacks me, then I'd say that's his fault. But if I'm being very lairy and putting it about and being provocative, then you are enticing someone who's already unhinged– don't do that. Come on! That's just common sense. You know, if you don't want to entice a rapist, don't wear high heels so you can't run from him. "If you're wearing something that says 'Come and f*** me,' you'd better be good on your feet... I don't think I'm saying anything controversial, am I?"
>
> –**Chrissie Hynde**, speaking about being gang raped at 21[2]

The real world. The man's world. The kind of world where women are trained to believe they are wrong, and to blame, when someone else visits monstrous violence on them.

Taking responsibility in this world means that violence against women is to be expected, and that the burden to prevent that violence belongs to the woman.

In this context, what does being "one of the guys" even mean?

I would love it if being "one of the guys" meant that I, too, got pay raises and opportunities based on my potential, instead of my having to prove my worth and merit.

I would also love it if "taking responsibility" meant calling out and taking action to reduce this ridiculous burden, instead of accepting it.

However, taking responsibility *usually* looks like finding strategies to work inside of the man's world anyway–ignoring sexism, doubling down on effort, and fighting forward. If you manage to get past all of the landmines in front of you–and you rise to the top (congratulating yourself on your exceptionalism)–who is raised up with you?

Trapped by False Meritocracy

Women do exceptionally well in environments where effort leads to success–similar to the school system, a meritocracy rewards diligence and good work. Unfortunately, that alone isn't enough for women to break into leadership or more senior positions.

The problem is that *women* are trained to perform as if the playing field is level, and that good effort will be rewarded, and that any failure to get past the glass ceiling can be attributed to a variety of things–but never an unfairly stacked deck. Just the other day, I had someone try to simultaneously deny the wage gap (women earn on average 75-80% of what their male counterparts do with the gap increasing with age), while explaining it away that women "want" to be able to go home to kids and family while men "must" be the primary wage earner. This, in 2016![3]

And if that sounds like "just a wives' tale" (see what I did there?) Check out what Microsoft's CEO has to say about women asking for raises:

"At the conference, Nadella implied that instead of asking for a raise, women should have faith that they will be rewarded over the long arc of a career. 'That... might be one of the additional superpowers, that quite frankly, women who don't ask for raises have,' he said. "Because that's good karma. It will come back."[4]

It will come back...*as what* exactly?

In my family–with two female wage earners–well, this kind of karma doesn't work out so well. Not to mention how this works for our many friends who have the same family structure, as well as children to care for. Of course there are many single mothers and single women providing for elderly or disabled family members while working. Even in heterosexual partnerships, women are more and more ending up as the primary breadwinner, whether they planned to or not.

Individually, women have to deal with a lot. It's worse when we can't even agree that there are clear problems entrenched within a system that we can't simply power through with greater exertion.

Bias—You're Soaking in It

"I'm not sexist/racist/homophobic BUT…" is a phrase that usually precedes some blanket statement about women (or African Americans, gays, Muslims–any group who isn't male or white) that is elevated to *fact* with its pronouncement–some generalization that makes their point, but relieves them of the responsibility to look at how their own assumptions and experience come from a place of entitlement and privilege.

It comes up all the time. Questions like, "How many women do we need to have a diverse workplace? We just hired a woman. Are you saying we need to hire less-qualified people?"

There it is. The assumption that the deepest talent, ability and potential can be found in an all-male hiring pool, and that letting in women or minorities is somehow watering down the stock. This puts women in the stupid position of having to prove we are just as good as our male counterparts (usually done by overachieving), so the proof is inarguable. We then must decide what parts of our talents we can bring to bear, because some things might come across as "too aggressive." It's like wearing an invisible backpack full of bricks on an uphill hike where you aren't just expected to keep up but also lead the march.

This leads to a variety of dysfunctions such as "impostor syndrome", the belief that your success is accidental and that eventually you will be "found out" as less talented or qualified than your results would indicate. This is especially potent if you are led to believe, overtly or covertly, that your mere presence on the team is watering down the stock.

Women who excel often find themselves isolated, having crafted a persona that has them doubling down on effort, while keeping the egos of their male counterparts soothed. While this might lead to success, it also sets them up for jealousy and recriminations from other women who haven't done as well. Indeed, the papers are full of female leaders that are looked at as odd outliers, and then picked apart for their failure to measure up to their feminine roles.

Carly Fiorina, Meg Whitman, Marissa Mayer, and Hillary Clinton–these are examples of women who have climbed to the top of their careers as leaders, notably in technology and/ or politics, and are watched with more than mere curiosity.

Regardless of opinion on their political or corporate lives, the media is focused on them as if waiting for the inevitable misstep that will prove they shouldn't have been in charge in the first place. Successes are regarded as novelty, while their failures framed as enormous over-reach. All the while, attention also goes to critiquing their looks, their family lives and structures, and seemingly their out-and-out brazenness to go further than a woman ever should.

What Does It Take for a Woman to Win?

November 9th, 2016: I had to take a day off from work—Hillary Clinton lost her bid for President in a stunning upset. My head and heart hurt. I needed to process what happened.

The prior weeks and months had been filled with me clinging to every news story, watching every debate, donating, calling swing states, blogging and hoping against hope that on this day I would wake up with a new phrase I could use—*Madame President*. But the three bottles of champagne we had chilling in refrigerator, set aside to toast the breaking of that highest and hardest ceiling, remained unopened.

I didn't get it. How could someone with 30 years of public service, who won every debate and who campaigned through pneumonia lose to an opponent with no political experience and who also bragged about sexual assault on a hot mic?

How could this happen?

Despite winning the Democratic nomination with a solid 12-point win over Bernie Sanders, Clinton was hampered by an enormous wet blanket of tepid support. While her opponent's supporters were intent on criminalizing and discrediting her, progressives constantly referred to Clinton as "the lesser of two evils".

It nearly gave me whiplash reading the variety of criticisms levied against Clinton. She was called a liar, crooked, a person with no stamina, a person with bad judgement, and a "nasty woman". She was also accused of having "hate in her heart" and was even threatened with jail time by her opponent.

Oddly absent in the media clatter was any significant challenge to the false rhetoric and blatant misogyny of the Republican campaign. Even so called progressives openly wondered if voting for the opponent would be more revolutionary than lending support to Clinton.

Despite the persistent negativity facing her from both sides, Clinton ran a disciplined campaign focusing on her 30 years in public service, her record in passing legislation and her role in advancing healthcare and services for children and families. She handily won all three debates and was praised by President Obama for being the most experienced and prepared candidate for president to ever run.

However, it seems being the most experienced and prepared wasn't enough.

The bar was far higher for Clinton than her opponent. Despite her opponent's lack of competence, lack of impulse control, racism, and general repulsiveness, how there could even be a question about Clinton's fitness to serve as President?

We enabled this outcome the same way we've enabled every other glass ceiling to persist: by discrediting powerful women, by failing to speak out against misogyny, and by encouraging women in general to tear each other down.

On election day, 53% of white female voters voted for the Republican candidate.

I wonder what those women saw in Hillary that they were afraid of seeing in themselves?

It's Kind of Cold in Here

Women see this treatment of the best among us and it chills us. We are tempted go back to our corners and tone it down. We don't stop longing for the corner office, but that longing coexists with the knowledge that powerful entities wish to stop us from being there, and some are more than willing to take us down for simply succeeding against the grain. The most powerful entity of all it seems is the willingness of women in general to mistrust and denigrate ourselves.

We let the insults pass—sometimes we believe them. We work harder. We hope that people can see our merits and not our struggles. Above all, we stay silent on the sexism–because pointing out the unfairness or the resistance will somehow be seen as asking for favors or exceptions or wanting more than we should.

I want to know: Why is it wrong for women to be on our own side?

Trapped in Our Stories

"There are events that divide our lives into before and after. I notice that most people, when asked to name such an event, cite something that gave them a feeling of emotional connection, whether it was witnessing a birth, or walking New York streets after 9/11, or viewing a photo of our fragile planet from space. Mine was an event you may never have heard of: the 1977 National Women's Conference in Houston. It may take the prize as the most important event nobody knows about. In three days, plus the two years leading up to them, my life was changed by a new sense of connection–with issues, possibilities, and women I came to know in the trenches. The conference also brought a huge and diverse movement together around shared issues and values. You might say it was the ultimate talking circle."

–**Gloria Steinem**, from *"My Life on the Road"*

I never heard of the National Women's Conference–I would have only been 10 years old when it happened–but by the time I got to college, the famous women that made this event alive were already relegated to being the subjects of "women's studies" classes. Feminism wasn't making the news anymore, except to say it was over and no longer necessary.

I attended more than my share of women's studies classes in school, and always wondered why it made my mother so angry! Getting together in a lecture hall mostly full of women– talking about the rights of women, women's history (and the suppression of it) and -*gasp*- lesbian rights–I couldn't talk to her about any of it. I was accused of wasting the tuition dollars she was spending. Even worse, I was engaging in some kind of perverse, stupid and *disobedient* behaviors.

I didn't get my mom's rage. Why wouldn't she be excited to see me so engaged in learning about my own power? Why wouldn't she be supportive of a movement that meant I could achieve things that in prior eras weren't even a remote possibility?

And then I got it.

A little about my mom here, she's brilliant. A polyglot with an engineering background, she survived the Nazi occupation of her hometown in Russia–a feat which included the experience of being thrown in a jail–and enduring daily interrogations for her possible ties to partisan fighters, eventually being shipped to Germany as slave labor.

After the Allies pushed the Nazis back, Mom was stuck in Austria, where she met my Dad, an American GI who courted her, married her, and brought her back to live in Texas.

There, she faced the culture shock of being an educated woman living the reality of 1940s Bible Belt culture.

Mom's life then became about adjusting to American life–her aspirations for achievement and adventure wholly replaced by watching my siblings at home while my father was on duty with the US Army. With her new culture, new responsibilities, and her new life, it didn't serve her to wish for, or mourn for, the more empowered life she remembered back home. Mom chose to dig into her new role, and made the best of it. She didn't see a lot of choice.

I came along as a "late in life baby." Even though my brothers and sister were now near adulthood, Mom once again had to defer her own career plans to care for little me. When *little* me became *big* me (in other words, an out lesbian with big opinions and no desire to fit in) it was hard for Mom to take. Feminism, especially embracing my queer self, looked to her like I was trivializing her life and her sacrifices. In her opinion, I should have focused on my studies, entered a traditional profession (something that makes sense to her, such as doctor, lawyer, or art gallery owner) married a brilliant and wealthy man (not a soldier), and lived a more graceful, easy to explain existence. Something that would make her proud, something that was possibly more reflective of the choices she wished she could have made for herself.

I am endlessly curious about Mom's early life, her experiences during the War, the occupation, and especially what she needed to do to survive. My mother has told many stories that make the past seem ok to her. So much *wasn't* ok. So much is still untold.

For years, I've lived as some kind of outlaw in Mother's eyes–it was the price of writing my own stories.

I never wanted to erase my mother's ambition, or negate her experiences, I just wanted to create my own.

The Dirty Little Secret That Keeps Us Stuck

Telling the truth has a cost. When we start telling the truth–and stop telling ourselves the stories that keep us safe where we are–it can *scare the crap out of us*. What seemed tolerable or "just reality" before, something we could not perceptibly change, starts to show itself as a drama we were covertly conscripted to support through unwitting complicity. We might be angry or feel used or abused when we come to this realization.

When women start telling the truth to each other, things start to happen. Things start to change. And that scares the crap *out of the world*.

This is what feminism is truly about: Women seeing clearly. Women changing the game.

We had little victories along the way (we can now wear pants openly, for instance) and some big ones (for the first time ever, a woman is the presidential nominee for a major party). Today, things are somewhat better in terms of entry-level opportunity and inclusion. Despite that, we still see life through the funhouse mirrors of gender bias which distorts small advances into "proof" that women are now on equal footing because men no longer run to open doors or dare to call women "sweetie" at work.

We celebrate women's victories, but just as quickly go in for the kill when other women fail to be perfect on all fronts. This is a dynamic that keeps individual women running scared and staying hidden.

The idea of an all-female board of directors, cabinet, or SCOTUS sounds laughable–and like "going too far"–and perhaps the underlying worry is that this would lead to decisions that aren't tough or practical. I mean, without a man in the room to make sure things don't go off the rails, everything could go to hell in a hand basket, right?

"In those days, in the Southern District, most judges wouldn't hire women. In the U.S. attorney's office, women were strictly forbidden in the Criminal Division. There was one woman in the Civil Division, and the excuse for not hiring women in the Criminal Division was they have to deal with all these tough types, and women aren't up to that. And I was amazed. I said, have you seen the lawyers at legal aid who are representing these tough types? They're all women."

–**Ruth Bader Ginsburg**

It isn't an accident that women remain divided and buy into stereotypes about themselves.

The effort to divide women–along color lines, along gender preference lines, along religious lines, along vocational lines–is deliberate. How else are existing power structures maintained?

We keep our discomfort to ourselves. We look past the problem, or believe we work our way through it without raising a fuss.

We forget that, as Martin Luther King, Jr. said, "Injustice anywhere is a threat to justice everywhere."

Our best efforts alone are defaulting to becoming the good girls who don't complain–and the highest praise available is to be the strong (and silent) woman who holds the world on her broad back *alone*. By looking away, we continue to allow the argument that this isolation, a divide-and-conquer approach that works against us, is our destiny.

We didn't get this far because we hid in our safe corners.

How about taking some justice for ourselves?

Efforts to bring equality to women galvanized at events like the National Women's Conference in 1977. "Because eighteen thousand observers came to Houston from fifty-six other countries, and because delegates were chosen to represent the makeup of each state and territory, it was probably the most geographically, racially, and economically representative body this nation has ever seen–much more so than Congress; not even close. Issues to be voted on in Houston also had been selected in every state and territory. It was a constitutional convention for the female half of the country."[5]

Not just white women. Not just wealthy women. A healthy representation of women from the many walks of life–*together*. And there they were talking to each other, building empathy and getting to understand that the problem one woman faced was a problem for all women–no matter where you come from.

Of course this was a frightening prospect, so churches sent busloads of their own loyal women who–under threat of excommunication in some cases–were ordered to vote *against* all measures that could bring the Equal Rights Amendment to pass. The ERA was a *big* threat to traditional family values (remember those?) and therefore it had to be stopped.

I must say the religious right was on to something–if women had equal rights outside the home, they might not be satisfied with "reality" as presented.

What other things are women unwittingly voting against themselves on? Are they "voting" for keeping gender bias in the workplace by acting as though they are one of the guys? Are they "voting" for 75% pay norms by waiting for that elusive cooperative karma to kick in?

I wonder what would have happened if those women on the church buses instead staged an open rebellion, joined the conference with open ears and open hearts, and started telling the truth of their own lives.

There is real power at play when individual women look to each other for support and stop trying to hold the world together alone. When we compare notes, tell the truth of our experiences, and start looking to each other for the help we need, the world needs a whole lot less glue.

Are you still wondering what feminism has to do with changing your exhausting life?

I'll break it down.

Feminism has nothing to do with proving women are equal to men. When we try to prove equality we are way off track.

This is the trap women get into when they silently shoulder every burden without questioning why things are set up so inequitably. The fact of the matter is, being as good as the best man is just as hard as being as good as the best woman. What makes this seem hard is the unacknowledged boatload of bull that women have to deal with (many times invisible even to ourselves).

Feminism has everything to do with having equal access to opportunities and freedom from fear of backlash and violence when we go for the things previously seen as the exclusive realm of men. Feminism is about removing the artificial burdens that come from a culture that favors men but pretends to be equal. Feminism is about being fair.

Want to be less tired? Get behind feminism.

You are strong. I hope you appreciate that about yourself. There is a real reason why you have been elected as the solver of problems, the glue in your communities and tribes, with broad shoulders that hold up the world.

When the going gets tough, you absolutely have the power to double down and muscle through. And you do. You know that complaining about your circumstances won't get you far, and rolling up your sleeves is the way to make things happen, or at least get out of the circumstances that you need out of.

Dedicated, determined you.

I know your impulse is to think, *It's a good thing too, I have so much to do!* I want you to stop for a moment.

There is a delicate balance to be struck between expressing your natural strengths and taking on the problems of the world.

The world has infinite need and will continue to pile demands on high and heavy–even if you give it everything you have. And the system is set up to keep you second-guessing yourself about your own worth and place in the world.

It sounds simple, but that critical monologue just runs quietly in the background at all times. Part of you is always coming up with a long laundry list of reasons of why your best efforts just aren't good enough. It's no wonder so many of us run hard and scared in the world. We are constantly bombarded with messages that our internal monologue is right, and that every time we attempt to go beyond what has been preordained for us, it is a recipe for failure and a hard, painful fall.

The feeling that there is no help for us, that we are alone and that we are perpetually on the brink of failure, keeps us stuck in a cycle of anxiety and exhaustion, keeps us separated from joy and the fulfillment of our dreams and purpose. There is massive cognitive dissonance in the belief that we are in a post-feminist world AND still living with sexism as a daily experience.

Instead of looking at the world with those critical, anxious eyes, look at yourself with eyes filled with compassion. You are enough. You don't have to buy back your worth through any great acts of strength. Your worth is intact, as is.

I know the challenges keep coming. Still, there are ways to meet those challenges without selling yourself short or doing ever more–in fact you will be doing less. A lot less! Many of the tools and strategies I share in the following chapters you can enact on your own. Others may require the support of a coach or another professional that can help you navigate through your choices when situations aren't so clear.

Bottom line: unless you are certain your ultimate purpose in life is to carry everyone else's burden, it's time to learn how to find your way out of your own strong woman trap.

Curious to see where you fall on the Strong Woman Spectrum?—take my online quiz "What's Your Strong Woman Rating?" at http://sashamobley.com/super.

Part Two

ESCAPING THE TRAP

CHAPTER 4

No is the New Yes

To start this process, I'm giving you a gift. Right in front of you, you have your very own "get of out jail *free* card."

If there is something you "have to do" today that you really don't want to do, this card gives you permission to not do it.

"But (that something or other you are dreading) has to get done!"

I hear you. Go ahead and take a break from the awful whatever today anyway. You get extra credit for putting it to the side if it is some stuff you are doing out of habit because of tradition, responding to family expectations, taking advantage of sales, obeying the phase of the moon etc. In short, this means anything that you are only doing because of external circumstances.

Experiment with seeing what happens if you step back. Notice what other people do or say. What are you thinking when you contemplate doing the thing? How does your body feel?

Unless something is going to literally blow up (if you are dealing with a gas leak for example), give yourself permission to put the yuck aside for a day.

Here are a few of my strategies for saying no (even to persistent loved ones):

I have a policy about… This has been more useful than I can express. For example, if someone asks you to lend them money you can come back with something like: "I have a personal policy against lending money to (friends, family, etc.)." You don't even have to explain why. This is a personal boundary technique that keeps things from getting personal when you assert them.

Another example where this works is requests for lending personal objects. ("I don't lend things out valued over $500," for example.) It's also useful when you are asked to run extra errands. ("I have a policy against handling other people's business around their kids, their home, their pets etc.")

I'm not the best person for the job… Ok, this one is going to test you. If you are constantly hooked by the experience of people leaning on your infinite competence, now is the time to share the competence with others. Case in point, when I was still working hands-on in IT, I would get unlimited requests for my expertise to fix minor to major computer problems. While I loved the acknowledgment, I found myself taking on things I had no idea how to fix and then getting stuck because giving up meant losing my "expert" status. I had to decide if I wanted to be an "expert" at fixing other people's issues, or have my time back for the things that were mine to work through in the first place.

I also learned to turn down low-paid and unpaid catering jobs, disguised as opportunities to contribute for other people's bake sales, baking cakes for parties I had no intention of attending, etc. I chose not to do those favors. They could get exactly what they needed from the bakery down the street. Flattering as it may be to be the top baker in mind for family and friends, I just didn't have the time. The next time you get caught in the "you're the expert" trap, give them a referral to someone who has the time and inclination, or whose business will thrive as a result. Everyone will be far happier for it.

Let me think about it... This is particularly helpful when people ask you for something big, and perhaps really meaningful, and they catch you off guard. When a family member corners you with some big ticket way in which they want you to support them, and you feel drawn in, it is far too easy to say, "Of course I will."

Saying, "let me think about it" instead buys you some time so you can compose yourself and give your most supportive answer that keeps you in integrity with yourself. Even if you do end up saying yes (not every big ask is a no), you can feel even better about your answer because you took time to think about it. It also gets people used to the idea that not every request they make of you is an automatic yes.

Above all, be brief and resist the need to over explain yourself with complicated reasons or back-stories. These are really unnecessary and just open opportunity for people to counter you with reasons why you should say yes instead. Saying you won't do something is far more powerful than saying you can't. For persistent people, "can't" only represents a challenge to get to "can" and get what they want out of you.

What if they REALLY won't take no for an answer? If you've tried the above things and someone is still badgering you, feel free to swiftly end the hostage crisis with a decisive no. I have found it helpful to imagine a boundary (a wall, a force field, a rubberized barrier) and just say, "I'm practicing saying no–thank you for the opportunity" and end the conversation.

When I give an answer that someone else doesn't like, I take a page out of Cole Porter's book–don't explain, don't complain. No is a complete sentence.

Where Is Your Resentment?

Resentment–when I work with my clients that word comes up a lot. It implies that something is on your plate and you are doing it, but that you wish you weren't. You may even *hate the reason* why you are doing it.

This comes up a lot when murmurs of *I'm surrounded by idiots* start to fill your head. You reasonably see what you have to do as something that *someone else* should do. And yet *you* are doing it.

This is the time for you to start practicing saying *no*. You can get some clues about what you can say *no* to when resentment starts creeping in. Listen to the story you tell yourself when you say *yes* to something. If you resent that thing, soon you start to see that it was probably something unnecessary for you to take it on–except for the fact that no one else was stepping up to do it.

One of my mentors sagely said to me once, "Your family can love you lots and *still* let you take care of everything."

Picture the family sitting in the living room, enjoying a movie, as you are still in the kitchen doing dishes–seething. It isn't even that you want to see the movie so much as that you're increasingly perturbed that the people in the living room can't seemingly see that you are picking up after them and washing their filthy, nasty dishes! Why don't they see that?

Resentment.

The truth is your family may actually want you watching the movie with them more than they value you making the kitchen spotless. The dishes still need to be done, but you are no longer the only answer.

Doing the dishes seems relatively trivial, I realize, but saying no when you assume something is expected of you is building a new muscle. We start with small things.

Instead of blowing a gasket, try this: The next time you find yourself the default answer for some responsibility that you would like see shared around, start experimenting with leading the action. For example, after the dinner and before the movie starts, you notice there is a daunting pile of gross, dirty dishes. Everyone is heading to the TV and here's your chance.

"Hey, can we all help get these dishes done first?" You might have to make some gestures to get people moving, but try it and see what happens.

Let's say they don't move, or perhaps they overtly say they're going to do it later (which they may or may not intend, you know your family). You can either elect to do the dishes then and there, knowing everyone else is electing to *not do* the dishes…. *or,* you can also elect to *not do* the dishes. The dishes will just be sitting there when the movie concludes. Notice who pipes up about the dirty dishes then, and how it comes up. Are they wondering why there isn't a clean cup? When they look to you, you can have a discussion about the dishes not being your sole job by default.

If you live in a household where there is a notion of "women's work," this is a good example on which to practice challenging that notion. It's not men's work or women's work–it's just the work of the group–and someone has to do it (e.g. not you every time).

Stage a Rebellion

I built my rebellion muscle early on.

Back in my twenties, I was partnered with a woman who was highly extroverted and loved the holiday season. To be honest, we were both into the holidays. We always had a decorated tree that we invited friends over to decorate with us. We went to parties, spent time with our families, and generally enjoyed the colorful fun of the season.

One year, all the visiting and spending time with others just burnt me out. After cooking two holiday dinners by myself to entertain my own family and friends, my lovely partner volunteered me to cook for her cousins, who were visiting her family. Don't get me wrong, these were lovely people—*and* I love to cook—but I noticed that with every thought about it, my entire body felt like I was wearing a lead suit. I just couldn't face another evening of cooking and socializing. I needed a break!

I chose to not go. I gave my partner a recipe card for my beef stew and told her she could call me if she needed advice, but I was going nowhere that evening. She wasn't happy about it, and her family wondered, "What's wrong with Sasha?"

I don't remember exactly what I did with my evening, but I believe it included putting my feet up and watching a movie. All I know is that when I think back on that night, and being willing to make that choice, my body relaxes a little and I breathe a sigh of relief.

Disobedience can be the most delicious thing ever. It can also save you.

Only a couple years ago, I had a manager who invited me to work on his team. I was super excited. We talked about plans that potentially included travel, and we projected how my experience would be used on his newly-created product development team. Once I came on board, he relegated me to the task of "communications." I was confused. This was an engineering group, and I had just come off a project where I was leading engineers in a data center migration. I also noticed the "communications" role was poorly defined, and my so-called mission was supposed to get the larger organization interested in what the engineering team was doing.

So, newsletters.

I had no interest in this position as it was actually drawn up. I had joined the team because I wanted to influence the direction of our platform. It wasn't a fit. But rather than say that directly, right off the bat, I decided to watch and wait. Maybe it would work out. Maybe he had a plan.

No, he didn't. His manager didn't understand my background, and had told my new boss he doubted my ability to work in such a highly technical environment. He thought I could bob along doing newsletters and editing PowerPoint slides for six months, and then they would revisit my role.

This was *not* going to work out.

Initially, I decided to be a good sport and give it a shot. I came to work daily but I struggled to find meaning in the work given to me. This was the first time in my long career where I had dared, switched jobs, and netted out with something that negatively impacted my organizational standing. It wasn't long before I recognized this arrangement was never going to work, and started actively looking for alternate roles.

Sticking it out would have been the absolute wrong thing for a number of reasons, chief of which, it was a big waste of my time. Moving on quickly was the best thing I could do. Not only for myself, but for my team, as I was depriving them of an opportunity to have someone else engaged in that role who might love it and have more closely aligned aptitudes and interests.

Scary? I know. We are taught to obey and that we should be grateful for what we have–especially when it comes to employment.

But what if it is absolutely wrong for you?

What does "sticking it out" give you?

If the job is getting done, nobody is going to solve your unhappiness problem. This is all yours.

What's the Story?

Resentment has a signature in my body. I can feel it. It's in my gut and it burns. It lets me know I need to deal with something–and sooner, rather than later.

Before, I would let it eat me up, and do lots of creative writing exercises in my head describing why I should be happy with things as they are. I'd come up with stories like:

"I can do this faster/better/easier so I might as well take it on (even though I'm exhausted)."

"(Name) is really struggling. I'll just do this (even though I really don't have the time)."

"Ugh, if I don't do this, no one will (even though it really isn't a big priority for me)."

"I'm the only one who can do this (and if I don't do this, everything will go off the rails)."

"If I don't do this, what will people think of me? (It might be that I'm lazy, incompetent, selfish...)"

The key to dealing with these stories is to question them. Are the actually true? Is there another possibility that might be as true or even truer?

Here are some examples:

"I don't know if I'm really faster or better at this task. I might be or I might not be. Even if I am, does that mean I necessarily should do this myself? Why does it need to be done by the person who is fastest, or who has the most skill? Is there maybe someone else who could benefit (e.g. increase their skill or their competency) by doing this task?"

"(Name) looks like they might be struggling. But if I take it from them, is it necessarily the best thing? What message does that send him or her? What can I do to help that *isn't* taking on the task? How can I support his or her development in an empowering way?"

"It looks like if I don't do this no one will (and maybe that is ok)."

"I'm the only one who can do this. (Maybe, but in a world of 7 billion people, how likely is this?)"

Does it suit your purpose to be the *one person*–meaning, is the task aligned with *your purpose?* If not, reconsider the thought about you being "the only one" who can do it. As unique as your position or skill might be, you didn't always know how to do it.

"I have no idea what people will think of me. They might not be thinking anything at all. They might be thinking about what to have for lunch. At any rate, is it any of my business?"

Before we even have all the facts about what is going on, our infinitely creative brain is already telling us what reality looks like. It's a good idea to question anything you are telling yourself if somehow it looks like you are heading into a situation that is going to suck you dry.

I learned how to question my thinking in a very systematic way when I was receiving my coaching certification. It is one of the top tools I use when working with clients to change behaviors that are rooted in outdated beliefs about their roles or responsibilities. Give it a try on your own the next time you find yourself spinning tales about the things you "have to" do.

Screw Approval Seeking Behaviors

Some of us live behind cover photos. Pictures of the way our lives *should* look if we are killing it, living epically, ruling the world. Behind the Pinterest board–covered with photos of your lovely home, family, vacation pictures, cute puppies and kittens–is your real life with you? Or are you racing to keep up with the beautiful imagery that shows we are *winning at life?*

I'm going to keep this last point short and focused.

Dump anything you think you "should" do, especially if you think it is going to turn you into a good example of _____ (whatever your approval-seeking lifestyle is).

What is approval seeking? Glad you asked. Think of it as getting third-party endorsement for how you are living your life. It is whatever you think you ought to do, be, or have–that you otherwise wouldn't bother with–unless it somehow proves to the world you are worthwhile.

Here are some examples:

Going for a law degree because your Mom was a lawyer and you want her to be proud.

Running a marathon/doing Crossfit/Ragnar to prove to the world you are a *badass* (even though you hate running).

Buying tons of things to decorate with when you don't have the budget, but are terribly worried about what people think of your sparse surroundings. (Oh my lord, look at those balloon valances.)

Getting a tattoo or piercing to show you really *are* a special snowflake unicorn.

Cleansing/dieting/fasting so you can fit into some outfit from high school and *prove* that you are still hot (and that the weight is just a transitory thing).

If you aren't excited to death about these things, and find you are only doing them because you want to be, or at least appear to be, something else—*stop!*

The same thing goes for things that drain our personal energy; things that we resent doing, and which bring us no joy when they are done.

I see people running around trying to be better/stronger/faster when their personal time and energy are being eaten up by things that are actually someone else's to deal with, have gone on too long, or frankly are just not important (perhaps to someone else but not to themselves).

I will level with you. It took me a long time to dump my own approval seeking behaviors (and I would probably still be on spin cycle if I didn't get some help from a coach).

Last spring, I went through an energy audit with my own money. (Money is energy; anything you have a supply of, and can be traded for something else, is an energetic exchange). I tracked down all the little things that were eating up my cash supplies (think: death by a thousand cuts) and took stock of my savings, my retirement funds, and what my money was spent on month over month. It was a very revealing and *empowering* exercise. After doing that, I was able to make some changes, which allowed me to spend my money more consciously, and left me with a lot more in my pocket. Now, even the luxuries I spend on feel like really solid choices, because they are aligned with what is important to me.

So it is with the way we use our other energies: time, physical energy, resources, emotional capacity, and yes, spiritual as well. You will never get to explore any of these dimensions of yourself in depth if you are spending all your energy constantly maintaining your image and seeking the approval of others.

It starts with getting very comfortable with saying "no."

CHAPTER 5

Feeling Strong, Being on Purpose

L et's start off with a little imagination game.

I want you to picture something that always floats through your mind when you are thinking about your ideal life. It might be a visiting a faraway country with purple mountains, their peaks obscured by cloudbanks, raptors circling over a thick forest. Perhaps it's finally writing the story of your family, rekindling your interest in voice lessons, or immersing yourself in Italian literature. It's something that you keep saying "someday" about, but you never quite get around to it.

Take in all the details of the thing–make the visuals as 3-D and multi-sensory as possible. See yourself soaring with the birds, suspended by a paraglider. Imagine the conversations you will have during the time spent researching the fascinating details of your immigrant ancestors, the sound of your own voice at your first recital vibrating with your own emotion, or the smell and feel of the copy of the Decameron you found in a Florentine book shop.

Imagine this thing taking up a home in your body–a precious part of you. It is *in* you and somehow it isn't complete *without* you, either. You have become *one*.

Now, imagine yourself in a doctor's office. You are sitting on the edge of a metal table, wearing a ridiculous paper gown. The doctor is serious. He is looking intently at an image on a computer screen.

"I have good news for you. We can get rid of your problem with a simple, outpatient surgery. Take a look at the screen."

He swivels the monitor in your direction. On the screen is a scan of your entire body. Right next to your heart is a form. On closer examination, that form represents nothing other than your "someday" wish.

"All we need to do is cut that mass next to your heart away. It will be gone forever and these feelings you keep having will no longer be a problem. You'll be free from that longing, and live to be 100."

On a scale of 1-10 (1 being *YES please take this annoying distraction from me* and 10 being *I'd rather die than lose this part of myself*), where do you fall on having your "someday" dream permanently excised from your life?

We all have something pressing on our heart that we ignore. Sometimes that thing is a 10.

I cannot say I've ever met someone who wanted a 10 to be surgically removed, but I have seen people wait for one to simply die off–cutting off the blood flow until it fades to nothing. That happens by all the daily things we take on that push our dreams into the gauzy future of "someday". What gets left behind is only a ghost image of regret and an unanswered "I wish…"

Recently, I attended a leadership conference with 2600 other women. We listened in awe to Mellody Hobson and Duy-Loan Le tell their stories about their journeys from youth in poverty to becoming leaders in their field.

As they, and the other speakers, took the stage, they all said very similar things about what helped them transcend their circumstances.

One thing stood out.

All of these women, highly accomplished women with families and responsibilities outside of their professional lives, have one thing in common. They *only* take on pursuits that are clearly aligned with their purpose–what they want to achieve and who they want to be.

Whether you are running an investment firm, leading technologists, or looking to make a difference in your community or family–or following your "someday" dream–you don't have time to waste on the inessential. You have to be always on purpose. And to be on purpose, you have to know your purpose.

Do you know what your purpose is?

Knowing your "10" desires is the first clue.

The second clue is in understanding your strengths.

What Makes You Feel Strong?

Years ago, I took the Strengths Finder 2.0 test. The results confirmed things I suspected were true but hadn't taken too seriously because I was trying to improve some other things that were important to my day job at the time. Having this data finally in-hand changed things for me dramatically.

People who perform at a high level are regularly engaging in the activities that are real strengths for them. Not just things they are *good at,* mind you–their individual strengths. You can be really good at something (like solving other people's crises and dealing with their drama) and still come away feeling drained and horrible. Ideally, a strength is something that combines your talents *and* your passions. (Perhaps you are at least passionate enough that you become good at something because you are just that engaged.) Those would be your 10s.

Passion is naturally energizing. This is pure science, folks. Our usual educational and performance models focus on improving the things we are worst at—the things that we usually have limited natural talent and/or a complete lack of enthusiasm for. And while I wouldn't advocate kicking out the day-to-day minutiae-management skills that you need to get by in life, you also don't need to focus all of your attention on them.

It's amazing the reserve of energy we have when we focus on the things we are passionate about (and align with our purpose). Time flies by, and we enter a state of "flow" where we are completely immersed and engaged in what we are doing. And because of that, we are working *in harmony with* ourselves, as opposed to *fighting* ourselves.

Can you identify your strengths? Do you know the difference between improving on a personal strength and trying to fix a weakness?

Take a sheet of paper and create two columns. On one column, write "Loved It" and on the other, write "Hated It." For the next few days, write down the things you do (not things that happen to you or around you, but things you are actually engaged in doing) in one column or the other. Of things in the "Loved It" column, notice what talents are you using, the circumstances around them, and how engaged/passionate you felt about them. These will be clues on how to engineer more of these energizing, meaningful pursuits into your life.

On the "Hated it" column, how many of those things are the very things you think you "should" be doing? Are they things you don't enjoy and/or struggle with—but somehow they are on your plate?

What are the reasons for these tasks or activities arriving—and staying—on your plate?

Is it there because you are "sticking it out" for some reason? I've worked with some people who doggedly keep signing up for things they didn't like doing, because they think they need to grow from them or "give it another chance"—like doing their own taxes, or Turbo Pilates. Some of them have adopted the notion that people who "have it together" do those things.

Who assigned those items to you?

Here is another imagination game.

I want you to picture in your mind that person in your life who exemplifies the phrase "has it together." Ideally, this is another woman. Now, imagine yourself now meeting up with her by chance, maybe while you are running errands or stopping for coffee. Somehow, during the course of conversation, one of the things from your "hated it" list comes up, maybe it's the Turbo Pilates. You admit, somewhat guiltily, that you stopped going. Then Miss Has-It-Together breathes a sigh of relief. "Oh, me too! I just hated it! Glad to know I'm not the only one!"

You might be shocked to find out that the so-called "Have It Togethers" fail to eat all their vegetables, file last-minute tax extensions, have an unused treadmill in their guest room, and would love to kick those things to the curb as well.

You will do everyone a service by dropping as many things from the "hated it" list as you can. It gives other people permission to do the same with their own hated "obligations."

Know your strengths. Say yes to your 10s.

Taking Care of You

This has to be a *Yes*. Even if you aren't totally clear on your purpose, if nothing else, you need to take care of you. I'm going to cut the crap on the difference between some sneaky, sanctimonious self-improvement bull and taking real care of yourself.

What I said earlier about approval seeking activities applies *doubly* to your health and well- being. Drop every so-called "wellness" ritual that is designed to somehow fix something you think is defective about you. Drop every so-called "self care" routine that's really in your life because someone said you *should*.

If you are losing weight because every time you look in the mirror you feel some kind of hatred and disgust for your body–*stop right there*. You don't have time for that crap. No one has ever improved their health through a regimen based on contempt or self-hatred. No matter how good the program supposedly is, you will defeat yourself eventually, every time, until you come to your own plate with a loving heart for yourself.

Exercise is important. If you get a charge out of extreme sports, and running five miles before dawn puts a bright smile on your face and a bounce in your step, congratulations and carry on.

Love to run marathons and do Ragnar? Awesome! Have a good time, and I'll see you at the finish line with a banana smoothie and a hug.

However, if when you lace up your shoes, you are telling yourself you somehow are going to master your disobedient lazy ass–*stop it right there*. No one has ever elevated their body to a state of strength and resilience by telling it the story that it is a disobedient beast that needs to be subdued. Usually that is how injuries occur. Running through pain, training until you vomit, or some other self-brutality is ridiculous. Science is also on my side–hurting yourself isn't a good idea for anyone. So, knock it off.

When I was in my twenties, it seemed like I could get away with working late hours, beating myself up at the gym, and then employing some highly questionable dietary habits to ensure my body was lean and hard. My health and mental well-being suffered on every level during that time.

Eventually, I had a mental and physical break down that took me years to come back from– just constant fatigue, depression, anxiety, weight gain, and real inability to engage in my life. I had an acupuncturist tell me, "You've burnt off all of your *chi* and you also have a *yin* deficiency."

Chi = life energy

Yin = the feminine principle in Chinese Medicine

But I still didn't get it. I treated my body as something that failed me and that I needed to "fix" by force. This feminine principle thing also wasn't ringing my bell. I wanted to get back to the business of ruling the world on my terms–*hard, fast, non-stop, push*.

I had to quit all that to regain my wellness. Wellness looks a lot different for me today.

So here is my short list of "wellness to-dos" which make a difference in my life as it is now:

I Rest Like A Queen

I seriously prioritize sleep. I am something of a maniac about making sure I have a dark, quiet room. I have been through a half dozen pillows to make sure my head is both well supported *and* cool (my pillow of choice? 100% buckwheat hull). Resting when I'm dead won't work for me, if I want to feel good during the day. This means saying "no" to some things. I would rather be really, *really* present, and not do everything, than sleepwalk through my life.

Also, I make time for napping. I used to say I *couldn't* nap, but I realized that what was separating me from taking restorative rest in the middle of the day was a scattered mind. I now use a little audio program that helps me quiet my mind so I can drift off. When I was chatting with a colleague today, he said that back when he was in the Navy, he simply trained himself to sleep as needed. He can nap on a moment's notice to this day (I want to learn this one).

I Like Food

I have abandoned all methods of eating that promise I can eat unlimited amounts of *whatever* if I cut out some other *major food group* (carbs, meat, dairy, anything yellow...). I would feel all smug about losing weight while eating bacon on bacon burgers, but then lose my cool when I wanted to share a meal with other people because of some variance that made life hard for everyone (feeling like I'm going to die because I really, really, *really* want pasta but there is some stupid rule telling me I can't, or whining about the restaurant choice because their menu cannot accommodate my special diet). Yes, I know I can ask for all that, but honestly, I just want to eat and not suffer over it. I don't have allergies. I just need nourishment.

This is what I do instead.

I eat less meat and more veggies, fruits, and whole grains. I choose organic when I can.

I still eat pleasure food. And I mean pleasure...as in...I choose to enjoy eating it. This is not the furtive snatching of a bag of something salty and greasy on impulse (and yes, I still love having chips). I just ask myself *how I will feel* if I eat something. Sometimes it's a green light with the chips, and sometimes the message is a clear *stop*. The point is, I'm driven by how I want to feel during and afterward. I find I eat less ice cream, but I still do have it when it feels right.

I started eating many of my meals with chopsticks because it feels more beautiful and the process of using chopsticks makes eating more leisurely. I also cook simple meals that feel inspiring to me. Food has re-entered my life as a creative endeavor that is more nurturing, not competitive, and less dependent on things being super-rich or highly seasoned.

My eating life no longer feels horrible. And I come away from the table feeling...peace– happiness, actually. My eating regimen is no longer an ugly, judgment-filled process, and that, all by itself, is very energizing.

I Want to Feel Good

Brain health. I used to suffer from serious depression and anxiety. The book that turned that around was *Making a Good Brain Great,* by Dr. Daniel Amen. Not everyone agrees with him, but this book made me look at the physical aspects of my brain health. It started me on a path of eating differently, and led me to look at overall nutrition as a big contributor to my mood and mindset. While I still have my moments, depression and anxiety are no longer ruling factors in my life. That is *huge*.

Alcohol and caffeine both fall in the pleasure bucket. I enjoy each of these in moderation. I feel lucky that I can. I find a little goes a long way for me now. I always ask myself how I want to feel, and let that make the choice for me.

Moving My Body

I gave up all aspirational exercise. What I mean by "aspirational" is that if it has "bragging rights" associated with it as a primary driver for my participation, then I give it a wide berth. I have injured myself more times than I can count by trying to "prove" I can do something in the physical domain.

Having said that, there is a fine line between aspirational pursuits and growth. We are growing beings—right up to the day of our death! This is why I still try things that aren't *easy*. I just gave up deadlines, self-hatred, and unrealistic goals around athletic performance.

And to make sure I am getting enough movement, I got myself a watch that tells me how much I do on any given day so I get *enough* movement. It has a snazzy green band and it politely taps me on the wrist when I've been sitting too long.

(I could stretch more...I'm working on it.)

Paying Attention Right Now

I employ a mindfulness practice that allows me to step back and assess what is happening in my life. Some of this is done on the cushion in the form of formal meditation. But often it takes the simpler form of stopping what I'm doing, breathing deeply, and then noticing what is going on in my mind and in my body in the moment. It keeps me from straying too far into activities that are off-purpose, or that could potentially use my energy poorly. It allows me to be selective and intentional about how I spend my time and energy.

Gratitude Changes Everything

I call gratitude the Master Energizer. It's a game-changer. Gratitude is a Yes maker. Possibility and abundance are revealed through gratitude. You see what you have, and honor the good in it. It's a deep breath for your heart.

The next time a situation arises that squeezes you hard and makes you want to retreat or escape, try this:

Get still for a moment and look around. Let things slow down as you notice all that is happening around you. Take a deep breath. As you feel the air filling your lungs, remind yourself of one thing you have to be grateful for. As you exhale, picture that thing in your mind. Feel its expression in your life. Let that blessing touch you. Notice how your body feels in that moment of gratitude. Do this cycle as many times as you can. Feel your energy surging with each new thing. Let it lift you and fill you with lightness.

Other tools. I integrated massage and acupuncture into my life long before it showed up in Oprah's favorite things. As I get older, I find these modalities are helping me traverse the fiery furnace of menopause, as well as recover from injuries. I also practice body awareness that guides my decision-making. I can literally feel, in my body, when something is good or not good. It saves me from my old habits all the time.

There are full books written on each one of these points, I suggest you check out the ones that pique your curiosity and explore the things that make you feel best.

But I'm serious about the approval-seeking thing. Kill it with fire.

On Purpose and Impassioned—Now What?

"Great," you say. "I'm stoked! But even with all this energy and purpose there are only so many hours in the day. Even with kicking a bunch of things to the curb, I still don't know how I'll get it all done. I just don't know how I'll get all these dreams I have online by myself. What if I get stuck again, and end up crushed by everything I *want* to do?"

Now that your plate is full of the good stuff, you want to get going. But how?

Hint: it won't be by coming up with all the answers on your own.

Curious to see where you fall on the Strong Woman Spectrum?—take my online quiz "What's Your Strong Woman Rating?" at http://sashamobley.com/super.

CHAPTER 6

Fast Train Out of Idiotville

One thing I say to myself when I'm in high frustration is, "I'm surrounded by idiots."

Terrible. I have a huge judgment against myself on this point because, of course, it's not nice to call someone an idiot (not even in your head).

Fine. But if you are surrounded by people who appear to be acting irrationally, non-resourcefully, and who have no apparent plan to deal with anything at all...well, conclusions are drawn.

The world then appears to be a kindergarten—where you are surrounded by children who need to be corrected, protected, and corralled—and you seem to be the only teacher in the room!

How does that make you feel?

Tired? Stressed? Like there is no escape? Is everyone looking to you for their next instructions, or are they waiting for you to simply bring order to the chaos?

There is one truth in this: People rise to the level of your expectations.

What if, in the sea of incompetence around you, there was another smart person?

No, seriously. Look out at the drooling, impatient children around you. In that crowd, there *really is* a smart person—at least as smart as you—waiting to jump into the fray.

The question is: If this person exists, why hasn't this supposedly smart person jumped in already?

The Case of the Totally Secret Obvious Answer

A couple companies ago, I was put in charge of a large engineering project. My own boss was a sweetheart of a man who ruled our team with a blend of tenderness and fury. We had a lab environment that was used for testing. The issue we faced was not having a consistently accurate report on what resources were available in the lab–we exchanged things all the time. Our boss wanted to be able to review things on a daily basis so he would be informed.

"I just don't know why the team isn't staying on top of keeping the lab occupancy. It's really *simple!*" He'd rage, and I'd agree, and we'd commiserate about the sad state of things.

I really wanted to please this guy, and I thought I knew the answer. I was going to step in and ensure we maintained awareness and carefully tracked everything going in and out of the lab.

I created a spreadsheet. I populated it with information we needed to track. All the team had to do was enter changes as they happened. Simple!

I published it, and I let the team know what was needed. They all nodded their heads, and said they would do their best to keep me up to date. I couldn't wait to show my beloved boss that we were on top of things (especially the part about how *I got things under control and made that happen!*).

Daily, I'd send the team polite notes, asking when they would get their updates in. The response was always some variation of, "Oh, I'm so sorry. I will get to it later today. I'm dealing with this other issue."

I'd patiently wait. I'd check the sheet. I'd check on them again. They looked busy, but not on the things that *I wanted* them to be busy doing. Not answering my request.

My patience would wane. I'd follow up with less-polite notes. Regardless, very few updates made it into the spreadsheet that way.

Was I going to have to ask them for each individual change and enter the information myself?

That's what it looked like. I was pissed. It seemed pretty clear that I had to do my job *and theirs* because they were either too lazy or just didn't care.

I went to speak with the person who made the most changes, and asked where I could access this information.

"Sure thing. Let me get that for you." With a few commands he created a report that had all the updates already integrated for the lab, it came directly from the system. It was nearly identical to what I had created manually, I would only have to make a few changes to make it presentable.

I was puzzled. "I don't understand why we aren't using this for the updates."

"I tried to tell (our boss) that, but he really wanted it presented in a different format. He could have had this, but he got frustrated with the format. The updates are automatic. He could pull this himself."

I quietly retired my own sheet, and just reformatted the report from the system.

I like to feel smart. I especially like to think I have the answer. I *really* like it when other people think I have the answer, too. You know what I like even more than that? *Results.*

The work place can be the perfect environment to challenge the idea that you are surrounded by idiots. It is very easy to listen only to the loudest voice in the room—especially if it is your own. There is a lot that goes unnoticed when you have your "idiot finding" glasses on.

Hey Look, Smart People!

It can be a major turning point when you start looking for the *intelligence* in the room instead. Not as a substitute for your own ideas, but to raise the IQ expectations for everyone involved.

You can turn around the idiot-seeking behavior by listening to your own thoughts. When other people talk, what are you saying (even to yourself) about them—the things they bring up in conversation, how they interact, or ways they show up at work. Do you mentally interject and stop listening? What are your judgments about them, and how do they color what you allow yourself to hear?

"Oh, I don't do that. I'm very open-minded," you say.

I hate to break it to you. We are judging machines. We can't help it. The brain is wired to make shortcuts of all the input we receive in order to further our survival. The problem is that shortcuts we might have learned in the past that were situational, or part of growing up (where we were still developing and surrounded by others that were still developing), that were *perfect* shortcuts for the time, are not good ways to approach the world today.

Unlearning these filters takes effort–and it can be done. You can start by questioning the things that you think are true about someone else. Here are a few examples.

"The guys aren't updating my spreadsheet–they are so lazy! They only want to do the things they are interested in."

Newsflash–I don't know anyone who wants to do things they aren't interested in, especially if there is a better, more efficient way to do it.

"Stacy won't be able to help you. She's from the inside sales team–she wouldn't know about _____."

Really? So good to know you have a total catalog of Stacy's life experiences. And even if she doesn't know the subject in detail, you don't know who else she might be connected to, what resources she uses, or what her interests are. People can often help in surprising ways without being "experts" or having all the answers.

"This is my problem to solve. Nobody understands it or cares as much as I do." Are you sure there aren't people around you who care just as deeply, and are looking for the way to express it? What if you invited them to?

Nearly everyone wants to feel smart and helpful. Think about how you feel when you are asked to step in and help in a big way. Giving someone that gift can be the greatest thing for them–allowing them to grow, lead, and experience validation for their gifts or their contributions.

Think of the first person who looked to you for your help and you were able to show them your secret talent. How do you feel when you think of them? How do you feel about yourself? You can give that to another person by asking for them to dig into their own talents and creative problem-solving abilities.

One of my clients shared a story with me about how a coworker surprised her.

"There is one person in particular that is my go-to resource for certain tasks. I knew if I handed him some work, it would be done perfectly. I loved being able to lean on him for tactical things, but I sensed there was more than met the eye with him.

I shared a lot of praise about him with his manager, but I suggested that it would be interesting to see him take on a more senior role that would allow him to influence the direction of how some of our products were deployed and tested, as well as some hand in design.

Later in the year, we all sat down to plan an exercise. I had my prior plan, which I knew would work well. I also had directives from leadership to mitigate effort and risk in favor of a different program that was using a lot of resources and had everyone in a frenzy.

Well, my go-to guy piped up with an idea that the rest of us decided against because of the risk. However he was really prepared with a plan on how to reduce the risk that we hadn't properly looked into. I encouraged him to give us more details and took notes.

Unfortunately, I "knew" that our leadership wasn't going to go for it, so I attempted to keep our original plan intact. But he persisted, and insisted that we bring this up to the leaders who had the objections, so they could at least understand what we could do and the potential benefit."

Short conclusion of this story is that in the end, she supported his idea to leadership, and they decided to run with it. The result increased the test value on several levels. My client's program exceeded its success criteria, which resulted in some nice recognition for her as well as her protégé. Everybody won.

I used to believe in something called The Lowest Common Denominator, the idea that intelligence sinks to the lowest level in the room.

This is what happens when individuals operate as if they are the only smart, committed, capable people present (and that everyone else is somehow working against them). Oddly, this mindset acts like a virus, upsets the group dynamic, and engenders an every-person-for-themselves attitude.

This isn't just about feeling smart. I imagine that at some time in your past, you were disappointed. Most of us have been. Think of a time when you needed someone to step up and they didn't. Who knows why? All you know is that you needed something from them, and they didn't come through. Your antidote, the one that has served you so well all these years, is to just buckle down and do it yourself. You get to control things. You know it will get done (or not) because you are handling it. Above all, you don't have to be disappointed.

The problem isn't just that you are (once again) over-taxed by what you need to do, but you are missing out on results that could be even better than those you will achieve solo.

How do you enable the greater intelligence in the room? Here are a few ideas.

Make failure a safe thing. People are more likely to share their ideas and jump in if they know there won't be a public beheading if things go wrong. If you have a hard time with this idea, it's time to ask yourself if it is safe for *you* to fail at things.

Keep it human. This is a favorite maxim from one of the companies I used to work for. Keeping it human means you are allowing for error, assuming that people are doing their best, and are acting with good intentions. If things don't work out, it probably *isn't* the result of them trying to sabotage you, nor is it passive-aggressive laziness. Are you keeping it human with yourself?

Suspend judgment. Bias clouds everyone's vision. We make snap judgments based on gender, race, educational background etc. (Yep, I'm talking about prejudice.) Look for answers from people you wouldn't necessarily go to, or think of first.

Share the fame. Point out what is right with others. Appreciation for other people's unique qualities and resourcefulness has a warming effect for intelligence. When you hear or see something good, let other people know about it.

It's really easy to unconsciously turn away the capabilities of others based on what you think they can or can't do. I, for one, didn't know how much this unconscious approach was limiting my own support structure at home.

Remember the story of that terrible, hot afternoon when I was sick in bed from Chapter 2? Turns out, Keri wasn't phased at all by the circumstances when she went in search of an air conditioning unit.

I fully expected her to return early, empty-handed and heat-stroking out. But she called me every two hours to check on me, and a few hours later she showed up fresh-faced and triumphant with lime popsicles, really fluffy, soft TP, and a giant fan that worked great to cool our room down. She nimbly assembled the fan while I sat immobile in a chair by the window with a lime popsicle. I couldn't move, so I couldn't help. She was ok.

Mom was ok, that day, too. The world didn't collapse.

Where in your life can you look at things with fresh eyes?

The intelligence is there. Look for it.

CHAPTER 7

Who is Coming Along With You?

Isn't it good to know the world isn't populated by uncaring, lazy idiots who need to be saved from themselves?

I know, eye opener.

One of the ironies of the digital age–an age that believes in its own ability to make the world more open and connected–is how little we actually talk to each other. How infrequently we truly connect and become present to one another.

If we weren't posting aspirational headlines about our fabulous lives on Twitter or Instagram, we'd be sharing pithy updates or sharing news items on Facebook.

So edited. So safe.

If you weren't doing those things, how would your loved ones ever know how you were doing?

I love social media and updates as much as the next person, but none of it replaces an actual human connection. In a sea of curated pictures, status updates, and carefully crafted online image making, it can feel pretty lonely for us bio-organisms–especially when we need help.

Several months after Steve's death, a longtime friend I hadn't spoken to in a while reached out because of her own tragedy–an ex-partner died unexpectedly in an accident. It shook her up. She asked to have dinner with me so we could talk.

We sat down, waited for the bustle of the waiter and busboy to subside, to get our drinks, to order a little food, and chit-chat about her remodel was going and my new job. There was a moment of quiet. And then she spoke:

"You know, I see you've really created something beautiful for yourself. All the women you coach with, the way they reached out to you. I could feel the love." And she looked up, her eyes a little bright. "I'm a little envious. It must be so wonderful to have that."

I let that sink in. Despite how difficult things were for me and my family that summer, many, many kind and wise people reached their arms toward me and held me up–in little ways and larger ones. Even though my new job was off to an unsteady beginning at that point, I already had my tribe.

And this is how you know them.

They want to know you. They also *don't have to be told what to do*.

When I talk about Tribe, it's not the way it's used in marketing where you might catch a dedicated audience of super fans.

The tribe I talk about is actually very small, very specific, very trusted.

But building a tribe isn't "I'll bare the most private parts of my life, and the people who are supposed to be in my tribe will just know what to do." That has a way of attracting voyeurs and emotional vampires–folks who may not treat your disclosures with the kind of tenderness they need.

It starts with building trust.

I like the trust model Brené Brown outlines in her book *Daring Greatly*–the marble jar is a system where people "earn the right to hear you." Every action a person commits in a relationship can either add marbles (behaving in trustworthy ways through acts of empathy) or remove marbles (actions that break trust with you–dishonesty, insults disguised as praise, failure to show up when they promised to, or lack empathy when the cards are down).

Tribe members should have pretty full marble jars.

I have people in my life that I have warm feelings for, but the marbles go in *and* out at an alarming rate. I like them and I wish them well, but they aren't in my Tribe.

Empathy is a word that is used a lot, but let's make sure we all have a baseline understanding of what that quality is.

Empathy is present when one person can deeply relate to or actually "feel" what another person is going through. It gives insight into how someone might want to be treated, or what they may need in certain circumstances. The "feeling" is what informs these choices.

When someone says, "I've been there," and then just listens, that is a clue that they have some empathy going.

Empathy isn't present when the person on the other end of the conversation can't relate to your problem and doesn't appreciate what reality feels like for you.

Our culture trains us to respond to people's pain with "something" but often it comes across as so uncomfortable and tone deaf that it feels worse than if nothing was said at all. The automatic "oh you poor thing" is thrown out so the discomfort can be acknowledged in some way but not to the degree that an actual connection is made.

This kind of pitying response is the last thing a strong woman needs. It's doubly awkward in that it's hard to admit needing some understanding in the first place countered with the unspoken expectation for things to get back to being normal again.

And empathy will know that when the garbage hits the fan, things won't be normal for some time to come. You need people who understand that.

Not everyone you know is going to have this kind of understanding. Discovering who does and doesn't is important information.

Getting your tribe in place is kind of a messy process. It requires something of us.

Vulnerability.

Yep. You have to put yourself out there and give people the opportunity to show up–or not. The inherent problem is that people are not always going to rise to the occasion. And it will disappoint you when it happens–because of who you maybe thought they were, because it will plain hurt to be let down, because you valued that relationship.

That isn't a license to shut people out and take over everything again (unless you are really interested in being the strongest, smartest person in the room...*which isn't working out so well for you anymore...is it?)*

Included in giving potential tribe members opportunities to show up for you, you also have to give them a chance to fail you. And then you deal with it when it happens.

If you are about to throw this book across the room, I understand completely. The strategies I lived my life by for some time were especially cultivated *because* I didn't want to give people the power in my life to disappoint me. At the same time, I didn't want to disappoint them.

Because, if you ask for help, well, *what good are you then*?

I don't know your story, but a round of pooptasia, wrenched shoulder, spider bites and getting thrown under the bus at work while grieving took me out of that illusion. I couldn't control everything. I had to let people rise to the occasion. I didn't have a choice.

And before you head into a full category-five life melt down, I want you to know that asking for help isn't just for special occasions, or moments of intense need. It is the best way to learn about who should be in your tribe. If you're not melting down, try starting with some small stuff.

Letting people do things for you sometimes doesn't mean people are saving you, or that you are somehow less competent. It just means you don't have to be the lone, strong force in your life. You can also choose to feel good about doing small things (and big things) to reciprocate.

I'm going to uncover an ugly little secret women live with. Many times, women are put in the position of having to prove that we can do it all so we can show our worth. And when it becomes clear that this is impossible, we hide in shame that *we* didn't measure up. This kind of thinking keeps us tired and keeps us stuck.

Asking for help is *a feminist act.*

Your Tribe is In On the Juicy Stuff

A few chapters back, I talked about understanding what your purpose is. You know that your purpose is the guide post to the most important, juiciest, most compelling things in your life. Anyone who is in your tribe should *absolutely* be in on those juicy, Level 10 dreams.

While they might not be experts in the *what* or *how* of your grand plan, the presence of your tribe is a synergistic and energizing force that enhances the whole process. They are not looking to compete with you, and they won't be trying talk "sense" into you when you share your crazy, wild, expansive vision with them. Even if they don't totally understand what you are doing, they know it is important to you, and they get behind you in small and/or large ways.

I have a few tribe members who publish newsletters regularly. I support them by reading them. I don't read every newsletter, but I'm sure to read theirs whenever I can. I don't offer feedback or other input unless asked–I appreciate them. For a writer, simply having your work read means so much. Any kind of critiquing needs to come from an extra trusted source– and it is *by invitation only.*

Did I just hear a collective gasp? About not just taking in whatever critique is sent my way? Does that mean I have some kind of papery thin skin that tears with the slightest contact?

No. I'm just really selective about who gets to give me a critique.

I earned a pastry diploma years ago, and one of our projects was to design, bake, and decorate a wedding cake. When you are fully professional and "in the business," you have many ways of making that process efficient. When you are doing it for the very first time, however, it is a multistep, multi-process endeavor that blends design, baking skills, architecture, and a steady hand to apply all those marzipan flowers and piped *fleur di lis.*

After I presented my cake, I was completely exhausted. One of my friends in class snapped a picture of me standing proudly beside it. I took it in to work to share around.

One co-worker showed up in my office and said, "Are you ready to hear about your cake?"

She then started, critiquing my use of color, lack of balance, and went on to tell me about her art degree and knowledge of color theory and blahdiblah…

Have you ever received unwanted criticism on the heels of trying something new, investing the effort and perhaps shyly sharing it? Were you confused about how you should feel–like you should be gracious in accepting this unsolicited feedback, when all you wanted to do was show off something you made?

Just remember this: You are totally allowed to ignore any and all feedback that comes to you from anyone that is uninvited. While this may not be true in all cases, it is true often enough that unsolicited feedback (especially the critical kind) comes from someone else's need to feel smart and superior. It does not come from a place of empathy or a genuine desire to be helpful.

We get told all the time that we should be more open to feedback. Some even say it's a gift.

It can be. Just be selective of the source. You get to do that. Really.

Who You Gonna Call?

I have a short list of go-to friends. I call them "bury the body" friends. We don't talk everyday but I know that when I need them, they are there (and will bring their own shovel).

But on the random occasion those friends aren't picking up the phone, I have some others I can call on.

Whenever I need courage to write something out, but I'm worrying about approval or how others will react, I remember Anne LaMott's words from her book "Bird by Bird": "Tell your stories. If people wanted you to write warmly about them, they should have behaved better."[6]

I turn to that piece of wisdom over and over again. It's like a friendly push in the back saying "go, I've got you covered". Most of the time it's exactly what I need when I'm worried my words will land in the wrong place and get me into hot water.

Many times, reminding myself of the things the people I look up to most have gone through gives me the inspiration and energy to do what needs to be done. I count them as my unseen advisors and mentors.

It's good to have these stand-ins, I can access them anytime. When I'm unclear on the justness of a situation I ask myself "What would Notorious RBG say"? When someone is coarse or disrespectful towards me or my loved ones I recall how Maya Angelou refused to have bigots in her home. Their collective wisdom keeps things clear.

Still, I really count on my real world friends.

Even as a confirmed introvert, I know I need others.

Let me ask you this: Do you treat reaching out to your favorite people as a special occasion? Life can be very busy–and the use of social media, while it's wonderful to help connect with a broad audience or reconnect with people from your past, lends itself to an extremely edited version of life.

> "If you want people to see you, you have to sit down
> with them eye-to-eye."
> –Gloria Steinem, *My Life On The Road*

Sitting down with others and seeing "eye-to-eye" may seem like a luxury–especially if you are busy and pegged with responsibilities. We turn to social media to keep up with others and to make up for the lack of time to connect. Unfortunately, this can lead to skimming the surface of life instead of connecting in ways that matter. We miss a lot of details when we don't look below the headline or photo caption. This isn't because we are callous–there is only so much we can process from a forum that is designed to hook (but not keep) your attention. Information flows by leaving many details–important ones–behind.

Get on the phone, book a plane ticket, get out your teapot (or your wine glasses) and get face to face with these important people in your tribe. Tell the truth. Listen to their stories. Make your life real and visible and be present for theirs, in all its real-time imperfection. It doesn't matter that there is a pile of papers on the kitchen table or hair in the sink. Time is passing–put your computer away and make the life connection.

The fact that your tribe is out in the world doing and seeing and experiencing the same real life challenges you are can be a big dose of courage for you.

Even your unseen mentors, no matter what their position is today, had many things happen in their lives to get them to where they are now–none of it is accidental. Borrow their courage. Read their words. Learn their stories. Listen to them speak. Let them be oracles that give you what you need at exactly the same time and place. Conjure their spirit in your own mind and listen for the perspective that their lens could give you on your own dilemma.

Does that sound nuts? We absolutely are connected. It's miraculous who you can call on even when they aren't in the room. Think of the smartest, most courageous person you can, and imagine asking them "what would you do?" Then listen for the answer. It could come in the form of an imagined conversation. It could come from something you just happen to read on your way to work. It could be something you overhear in a crowded coffee shop. The intelligence is everywhere for you to tap into.

Being a strong woman holding the world alone on your shoulders will keep you *in one place.*

Being one of the guys will keep you playing *someone else's game.*

It's time to find and build *your* tribe.

It's time to start writing those invites.

Curious to see where you fall on the Strong Woman Spectrum?—take my online quiz "What's Your Strong Woman Rating?" at http://sashamobley.com/super.

CHAPTER 8

Oops! I Forgot to Create My Reality!

I want you to take a moment to imagine the world when the weight of it is off your shoulders.

The world where instead of having all the answers, you have access to the answers you need.

The world where instead of isolating, you connect.

The world where instead of straining, you are strengthened.

The world where instead of holding it all together, you are held.

Take it in. Breathe it. Savor it.

Feels good, right?

And then you are back in the world you have right now!

The world full of idiots, needy people, and disappointments. Or is it?

Here is the thing. Once you start showing up differently in your life, other people start behaving differently as well. The thing is, you are *really* used to behaving a certain way. You've been trained by your family and your culture to behave that way, and you've been rewarded for it.

The corollary to that is: *everyone else* in your life is used to you acting a certain way, too. You've trained all the people in your life to expect certain kinds of behavior from you as much as you have been trained (and rewarded!) to handle the world's problems.

It's tempting to think this would all be so much easier if you just had smarter people around you, or if people would just handle their own garbage.

Also, if you are addicted to approval and rewards (like resounding choruses of "You're so strong! What would I do without you?") for being everyone's super woman, you are going to face some challenges when you are presented with the very situations that left you so tired and resentful in the first place.

What kind of rewards can you expect when you aren't a super woman? Who will you be in a world where other people are strong, capable, and resourceful? How will you feel when you are no longer everyone's go-to? These are all good things to ponder if your identity is built around being a strong woman.

Shifting your identity can be uncomfortable. It can create anxiety when you turn down things that were such reliable ego boosts before. It's a little like taking a job offer for something you know you won't like, or that doesn't pay you what you are worth. The creeping belief that this is all we deserve hovers over us and plays on the fear that we are only worthwhile when we are over-performing, over-delivering, and overextending ourselves for the benefit of everyone else—never mind what it costs us in time, resources and energy. This is particularly hard for women who historically have played a supporting role in the narrative of Other—the nurturer, the girl Friday, the one "standing behind." Those cultural imprints are hard to buck.

The truth about learning new approaches, habits, or ways of being is that learning them isn't enough. They need to be put into practice. And putting them into practice leaves the door open for lots of potential pitfalls. Here are a few that I see come up a lot:

We Liked You Better the Old Way

While it is true that many people will want to support you once you make space for it, some won't. Actually, it was really convenient for them when you were carrying everything on your broad back, coming up with all the plans, and generally dragging them by the hair through life.

How do you think they will respond the next them they soggily flop in your direction looking to be rescued from whatever conundrum they find themselves in?

"Oh no! If you don't help me I'm going to lose the farm!"

Never mind the fact that the mortgage company has been calling them for months to make arrangements. Never mind the fact that some earlier action on their part could have absolutely changed the current circumstances. If you (yes, you specifically!) don't help them, *they are going to lose the farm.*

And then your inner good girl kicks in and she whispers sweetly:

"Don't be so hard on Doofus…the last few months have been very distracting for her/him and don't you think you are being just a little more than judgmental? I mean, this could happen to anyone, right?"

So, guilt kicks in. *Big time.* I mean: Doofus is going to lose the farm. If you don't act, *Doofus is going to lose the farm!* You will feel this urgency in your entire body.

You start to reach for your Visa, but at the same time, your gut twists (or you feel whatever is your specific bodily sensation when a wave of resentment comes up).

Stop right there! It's time for you to put the brakes on this rescue mission.

Is it true that Doofus will lose the farm if you (yes, you specifically!) don't help?

What are alternate things that could happen?

Here are some possibilities:

Someone else helps Doofus.

Doofus gets a little more resourceful and figures something else out (alone or by putting her/his head together with other people... maybe even you).

Doofus loses the farm.

Oh no! Doofus lost the farm! She/he then reminds you that if you (yes, you specifically!) had helped her/him, this wouldn't have happened.

When this kind of thing happens does "help" actually mean "rescue?" Is that something they are actually asking for, or something you are assuming is needed?

Help doesn't necessarily equal a rescue.

The next time this scenario (even with smaller stakes) turns up, imagine what "help" would look like if it weren't an automatic rescue situation. How would you feel, and how would the person asking for help be afterwards, if a rescue is transformed into an opportunity for them to be resourceful?

Even if you believe they *won't* or *can't* do something, how would the dynamic shift if the help you gave empowered them to *act* instead of enabled them to *stay stuck*?

These are the types of questions you must answer in order to escape the Strong Woman Trap. And answering them (and sticking by your answers when pressed) isn't always easy.

Deathbed Promises

I'm sure we've all read a story about someone who on their deathbed has a final request, something important they are entrusting to a favorite relative or close friend to take care of after they are gone.

Maybe your specific scenario isn't exactly the same as this, but there are times we are elected to be the one to take care of something. We decide to take it on because being asked implies all kinds of trust and love and specialness. It's really hard to resist these requests. Some of these high-stakes requests might be...

Being asked to be a bridesmaid, or maid of honor, even though you can ill afford the dress, the parties, or the fact that your friend has elected to do a destination wedding in Tahiti.

Being asked to always "look after" you little sister/cousin/ne'er-do-well uncle (with the details of what "looking after" means left open-ended).

Getting elected to a volunteer job (secretary/treasurer/figurehead of the Floral Arrangement Society) when you actually are already pegged for time.

Making sure Great Aunt Sophie never has to live in a place that smells like canned soup and humanity.

These are all great requests and certainly important to the requester.

As the requester gazes into your eyes pleadingly, the temptation to say an automatic yes is right there. It's probably pretty overwhelming.

It's really hard to say no to someone you love.

But the fact of the matter is that you (despite your résumé of being super-responsible and resourceful) might not be the right person to handle this—maybe not as they envision it, maybe not alone and unsupported, and maybe not at all.

Even as you imagine all the ways you can fulfill this request, it still might be too much to take on.

There is something there urging you to say yes, isn't there? A belief, perhaps?

Good girls don't disappoint loved ones/friends/grandmothers, especially when they are putting their absolute trust in you and expect you to say yes.

So what do you do?

That's when you say: "Cut!"

It's time to get curious. It's time to use your empathy.

What would it feel like if instead of rushing to saying "yes" you held space for something different to come out?

What if you said: "Wow (insert name of friend or loved one), that is really big. I don't know. I need to think about it."

And do think about it. If you promise to do something you don't intend to do, everyone will suffer.

Instead, offer support you know you can give. Here are some potential responses:

Destination Bridesmaid–"I am so touched you included me. I have to think about this. I want to honor your special day but (the dress, the travel, the time commitment) might not work for me and I only want to say yes to things I know I can do. Know that I love you and will give it my full consideration."

Guardian Angel of Uncle Ne'er-Do-Well–"I'm concerned about Uncle Ne'er-Do-Well, too. What does 'looking after him' entail? Do you know what kind of support they need? Maybe we can brainstorm over some strategies. Does he know you are concerned about his well being in this way?"

Figure Head of the Floral Society–"I am so honored you thought of me for this post! You know how I feel about (whatever club or institution this is for). I have to think about this before I commit. I know this will require my time and attention, and

I only want to say yes to things I know I will be all in about. Thank you for considering me! I will let you know soon."

Keeping Great Aunt Sophie safe in her old age–"Let's get the rest of the family in on this conversation. We all need a plan for this time in our life."

Even if, in some scenarios, you actually are the best person for the job, it's really important to know what you are signing on for and that *you* have all the support you need to follow through. Being a secret superhero won't serve anyone long term.

Disappointment

You've put yourself out there and shared something really important and vulnerable. And the person you hoped would know what to do or say–well, let's just say you guessed wrong.

From time to time people are going to say and do stupid or insensitive things, this is as common as dirt.

Even your closest tribe members occasionally are going to get it dead wrong. It could have been a gaffe or a lapse in judgment. Still, it hurts.

I would be lying if I said I never took things personally. I do it all the time! I'm sure if there were a "Resentment Olympics" I'd get all the gold medals.

However, staying there and letting a story develop about how this person never cared about you, or that they are a jerk that is trying to ruin your life, is not a very good place to stay.

How you deal with these situations on the backend is where the opportunity is. It's time to get curious.

Many times our conflicts with others arise because we don't clearly articulate our needs. This is especially difficult for women because we are trained from an early age to take care of the needs of others before our own.

When I was having issues with a peer last year, my mentor shared a technique with me called Non-Violent Communication (created by Marshall Rosenberg). It's a method that allows you to say how something affected you without accusing or denigrating the other person. Here is the model:

When I see or hear (the thing they said or did that set you off), I feel (emotion) because I need (whatever it is that you need to know or feel when you are with this person). Would you be willing to (whatever it is you need from them that is different)?

This model takes the heat out of conversations and gives the person on the other end a chance to respond without all the defensiveness that could otherwise come up. It's an excellent tool to have when misunderstandings come up. You might even save a few marbles this way too!

Frenemies/Toxic Turd Buckets/Genuine Jerk Faces

These people seem to be "like friends" in that you go out to dinner or other events with them, but somehow, despite how funny or charming they may act, you come away from being with them feeling like garbage.

We explain away their behavior. "Oh, that's them just being them." You find the conversations are very one-sided, and when you finally get a turn to talk, often you are cut off mid-sentence. Or when you share something important, or that you are excited about, they quickly turn the attention back on themselves.

They might say subtle undercutting things, or just out and out mock you, quickly following up with "just kidding."

You start to share your new fascination and they quickly tell you about how they already know all about that, and how now they are doing something else infinitely cooler.

The quality of your interactions with this person seems to be heavily influenced by their mood, especially when you are alone with them.

This all feels confusing because these behaviors are mixed with a fun personality or other friendly behaviors that made you want to spend time with them in the first place. When you get sick of their crap and start to drift away, this person turns up the charm and you forget about the last time you came away feeling like garbage.

While this person might need a whole passel of personal growth opportunities (and possibly has a personality disorder), it is not your job to be the one that takes them down the path to self-awareness. You actually don't have time for that.

When you stop responding to requests for your time and attention, toxic turd buckets are going to pull out some major stops to get back in the middle of your field of vision–Grade A manipulation in some cases.

I'm giving you permission right now to not deal with them at all. It's okay, really. You don't have to talk to them, go to their kid's birthday parties, or even be Facebook friends with them (also, don't they always send those Candy Crush invites? Annoying).

Here is my point: Frenemies and Toxic Turd Buckets are usually the ones that put a few marbles in the jar, but then empty the whole thing out with some extreme act of narcissism or other self-serving agenda.

For example, if you reach out to someone after a major life event happens and they get back to you two months later saying, "Sorry, it's been really too long but I've had so much going on! For example, there was a squirrel in my chimney for three days!" This is a sign they are a Toxic Turd Bucket.

I would just take the marble jar back at that point.

We all want to be elected for our genuine good qualities. We want to be recognized. It is very tempting to say yes to any evidence that we are the person we hope to be–and sometimes those yeses turn us into unwitting participants in someone else's psychodrama.

Mind Your Business

One last thing, real quick.

To paraphrase Byron Katie, there are three kinds of business: your own, someone else's, and God's (or the Universe, or science…whatever runs your reality). You are only in charge of your business. This includes:

Your happiness
Your health
Your security (job, money, place to stay)
Your spirituality

Anytime you try to fix any of the above for someone else you are straying out of your own business. Just like the scenario with Doofus losing the farm, it's not your job to save other people or make them happy. Keep this in mind the next time you get pulled into gluing the world together.

Don't Go It Alone

The first few times you are faced with one of the well worn scenarios you used to automatically say Yes to, the urge to give in and save the day is going to show up. This isn't a failing of character–your neurology is wired for the automatic Yes from years of your socialized behavior. Get support from a trusted tribe member, or get a life coach in your corner, someone who can be there with the right tools and guidance to make your new habits stick.

I frequently work with clients who make the transformation from "knowing" something needs to change, to living lives they couldn't even imagine before–which is something that is hard to accomplish when the only person invested in your transformation is you.

When other people see the change in you, their behaviors will change too. That can show up as them meeting you as a true partner, or it can be them going off to find someone else to solve their problems. It can feel like true acceptance or a painful rejection–often the latter more than the former, which is why most people who truly want to escape the Strong Woman Trap need a coach or mentor by their side through the transition.

Either outcome starts with you.

AFTERWORD

If you were going to write fiction about someone you admire and look up to—someone you don't know but follow closely—what would their story look like?

We think we know people based on what we see. We assume certain things about them—how good they are at scrabble, how clean their house is, what kind of parent they are, and especially how they quickly and efficiently they deal with life's difficulties. Everything looks a little better than reality. We expect our hero "has it together."

In May 2015, my colleagues and I learned that our COO, Sheryl Sandberg, suffered the forever life-altering tragedy of losing her husband unexpectedly during a family vacation.

She asked for understanding and some privacy as she spent the next thirty days in sheloshim (formal period of mourning for a spouse in Judaism) and that she would be returning to work then.

Immediately, all the message boards lit up with kind words of support–the sort of things you want to hear when unimaginable tragedy strikes.

Again and again I heard people resound, "She is so strong."

My heart twisted and I said a prayer on her behalf that, of all times in her life, she be given the space to "not be strong."

This news of this tragedy came less than a year after my brother Steve's suicide. I was still picking up the pieces of my own life and fully conscious that "being strong" was a strategy that wasn't working–at least not my concept of it at the time.

During that horrible year, my life fully broke apart. "Being strong" and pretending that I was over the debilitating effects of my grief left me alternating between lashing out and sobbing alone in my car.

I didn't want that for Sheryl–especially with so many eyes focused on what she would say or do next.

When she returned, she penned a thoughtful and eloquent Facebook post about the first thirty days of mourning and her reflections on that experience, as well as how life looks now as a widow–having to go with "option B" and make the best of that.

I originally wanted to share her post in its entirety (it's lovely, truly) but it's easy to find on the Internet (simply search for Sheryl Sandberg mourning post—it comes right up). I encourage you to find it and read it for yourself.

I read it and I learned from her. It's nice to be able to say that and really mean it.

How did this one hero of mine deal with life altering tragedy?

With difficulty.

With pain.

With loneliness.

With awkwardness.

With humility.

But never alone.

We are destined to meet grief, it's part of our mortal experience. However, it was a revelation to me to see how taken by grief Sheryl was—and how she let herself be in that place, moment by moment not knowing how long she would be there.

Her story struck me with its infinite humility, her willingness to not insist on getting back to a normal that would never exist again, embracing help even though it was a departure from how she was used to showing up in her many roles both personal and professional. It was her turn to receive.

My prayer was answered. And still she is strong.

In writing this book I hope to give a kind of breadcrumb trail of stories and practical steps to refer to when everything seems to depend on you and the world isn't stopping to give you a break.

The core of it all is that we need each other and it is in best interest of all to enable others to be as strong as you are. Let others surprise you with their willingness to help. Let their strength be your own. There is no cultural norm so worth clinging to if it keeps you separate from the life you are meant to live.

You are more than just the glue of the world.

Your life is precious.

Find the right people to spend it with.

Find the right things to spend it on.

Let go of the rest.

The End.

ACKNOWLEDGEMENTS

Many talented, loving, wonderful people enabled me to devote time to writing and editing this book. Writing The Strong Woman Trap wasn't a solo act, and I wouldn't have been able to cross the finish line if they didn't show up for me in the many ways they did. So, some thanks are in order...

My wife, Keri, who showed up as my superhero time and again, supporting me and giving me time and space to work on this project.

My Mom, who shared all her life stories with me (as well as the gift of life). Your baby bird is flying!

My sister, Valerie, who constantly inspires and challenges me.

My brother, Mike, who is always there for me with his special brand of love and kindness.

The Amazing Andrea, who supported me through all my computer related chaos and did so much to enable my journey through the world of technology.

Christine Erickson, who has the eyes of an eagle and the heart of an angel.

Sherold Barr, who asked all the right questions and talked me off the ledge with loving kindness.

My editor, Kate Makled, who is the most talented editor I have ever known. You helped refine my thinking, my prose and you just get it in general.

John Matthews who is a total wizard.

Pantsuit Nation—thanks for reminding me what we are fighting for.

My Facebook family–thank you for letting me play with you every day.

The Martha Beck Tribe–you helped me start this.

Angela Lauria–you rock my world.

ABOUT THE AUTHOR

Sasha Mobley is a certified life coach and author of *Agile! The Half-Assed Guide to Creating Anything You Want from Scratch—No Experts Required!* as well as *Sylvia, Sylvia So Fast Sylvia*, and *Sylvia, Smarter than the Teacher*. When she isn't writing or working with clients, Sasha can be found enjoying the charms of the California coastline, experimenting in her kitchen, paddle boarding, or chasing whatever curiosity has her attention in the moment. If she's not doing those things, she's probably roller-skating with scissors or encouraging other disobedient behavior. Sasha lives in Silicon Valley with her lovely wife, Keri, two dogs, and three cats.

THANK YOU

It's one thing to read about escaping the Strong Woman Trap. It's another when you get dropped back in your real life and everyone is looking to you to save the day!

That's why I condensed the three most potent tools from this book into a download you can reference anytime. Go get your copy of **3 Tools Every Strong Woman Needs** from my website, http://strongwomantrap.com/. You can pull these out the next time you find yourself as the only answer to someone else's problem-use these tools for some on-the-spot help while you learn to shift away from old stories and make real changes in your life. Trust me, those tired situation are going to raise their ugly heads soon enough–keep these tools close by, okay?

Curious to see where you fall on the Strong Woman Spectrum?—take my online quiz "What's Your Strong Woman Rating?" at http://sashamobley.com/super.

NOTES

1   http://www.computerworld.com/article/2540912/
data-center/emc-denies-sexual-harassment--bias-charges-in-
lawsuit.html

2   http://www.huffingtonpost.com/entry/chrissie-hynde-
sexual-assault-controversy_us_55e44b9de4b0aec9f353b9c6

3   http://www.aauw.org/research/the-simple-truth-
about-the-gender-pay-gap/

4   http://money.cnn.com/2014/10/09/technology/
microsoft-ceo/

5   Gloria Steinem, *My Life on the Road*

6   Anne LaMott, *Bird by Bird*

Morgan James
Speakers Group

↗ www.TheMorganJamesSpeakersGroup.com

We connect Morgan James published authors with live and online events and audiences whom will benefit from their expertise.

Morgan James makes all of our titles available
through the Library for All Charity Organization.

www.LibraryForAll.org